How May AI Help You

OrangeBooks Publication

1st Floor, Rajhans Arcade, Mall Road, Kohka, Bhilai,
Chhattisgarh 490020
Website: **www.orangebooks.in**

First Edition, 2025

ISBN: 978-93-6554-151-9

Price: Rs. 399.00

Printed in India

HOW MAY AI HELP YOU?

THE ART OF PROMPT ENGINEERING FOR AGILE TEAMS

SANJIT BHATTACHARYA

OrangeBooks Publication
www.orangebooks.in

PREFACE

The Symbiotic Ascent:

The convergence of AI and Agile is fundamentally reshaping how teams operate and innovate. This powerful synergy augments human capabilities, automates tasks, and provides unprecedented insights for informed decision-making across industries. AI's ability to analyze vast datasets offers Agile teams granular understanding, enabling refined user stories, anticipated bottlenecks, and optimized workflows.

The flexibility of Agile finds a strong ally in AI, particularly with LLMs assisting in documentation and code generation. This evolving landscape highlights "Prompt Engineering for Agile Teams" as a crucial skill. The historical trajectory of AI, from early aspirations to recent advancements, underscores its intrinsic alignment with Agile's core tenets.

The synergy between AI and Agile is not merely theoretical; it is increasingly being validated by concrete data and real-world applications. Consider the burgeoning market for AI-powered DevOps tools, which automate infrastructure provisioning, continuous integration, and continuous delivery (CI/CD) pipelines.

According to a report by Grand View Research, the global AI in DevOps market is projected to reach $48.3 billion by 2030, growing at a compound annual growth rate (CAGR) of 21.5% from 2022. This staggering growth underscores the increasing reliance of development teams on AI to streamline their processes and accelerate delivery cycles – core tenets of Agile.

Furthermore, AI is revolutionizing the way Agile teams understand and interact with their users. AI-powered analytics tools can sift through vast amounts of user feedback, social media data, and usage patterns to identify emerging trends and unmet needs. This data-driven insight allows Agile teams to refine their product backlogs, prioritize features based on actual user value, and even predict future user requirements with greater accuracy. A McKinsey report on the state of AI in 2023 found that organizations that have fully integrated AI across their enterprise functions report an average increase of 12% in their profit margins. While not solely attributable to Agile, this figure highlights the significant business impact of leveraging AI's analytical capabilities – a capability that directly enhances the data-driven decision-making at the heart of Agile.

LLMs enhance Agile teams by generating code snippets for repetitive tasks, freeing developers for complex innovation. They also aid in refining user stories for clarity and alignment. Tools like GitHub

Copilot demonstrate the tangible benefits of AI assistance in daily Agile workflows.

However, integrating AI presents challenges. Organizations must address ethical considerations, data security, and cybersecurity. Varying perceptions and adoption rates among team members, influenced by integration and intrusiveness concerns, also need attention.

To fully realize AI's potential in Agile, organizations must foster a culture of trust and open cooperation. Leaders with strong emotional intelligence are crucial for aligning AI deployment with ethical values, ensuring positive team dynamics and preventing bias. Transparency in AI operations is paramount for building trust.

I am often asked, "Is AI going to replace Agile?"

This thought amuses me. It's like saying, "Oh we have JAVA now, we need Agile no more".

Come on, think what you are saying!

My friends, AI is a technology and Agile is a way of working, it's a thought process and a mindset. AI is not here to replace ways of working but to make it even more efficient and curate new complimentary ways to further empower the already strong Agile frameworks and methods.

The data and trends clearly indicate that AI is not a peripheral technology but is rapidly becoming the foundational layer upon which future innovation and efficiency will be built across all industries. As we move forward into this AI-augmented agile world, one fundamental truth remains: **AI is not going to take away your job; someone using AI will.**

Thanks to my parents for the value system that I have in me today, which inspires me to push myself increasingly every day and help people in whatever way I can. A big thanks to my wife, Devika for her unwavering love and the support she has been to me. She happens to be first level content editor and the brain behind the name of this book. And to my lovely daughter, Tiasha for being my biggest cheerleader and the sunshine of my life.

A loud cheer to all thought leaders, inspiring bosses, and speakers from all over the world who taught me think out of the box and from time to time helped me realize things about me which I could not see myself, especially to Ajay Kabra, Meetu Singh, Sandeep Bandhu, and Gagan Verma. I wouldn't be the person I am today, without you.

Thanks to Google, for the Gemini tool that has been extensively used for prompt validations, trials and content improvement and some screenshots for this book.

I urge everyone to treat this as a workshop. Go step by step and practice prompting with various logics, structures and templates provided in this book, alongside reading it. That would help you make the most of this book.

Table Of Contents

Part 3

Advanced Prompt Engineering

Part 1

Prompts and You

Chapter 1

Introduction to Prompt Engineering

Agile product teams at PepsiCo cooked up innovation with AI as the hero ingredient. The company employed generative AI and deep reinforcement learning to experiment with the shape and flavour of *Cheetos*. By building a digital simulation of the production process, PepsiCo was able to optimize product development cycles and deliver solutions that met customer preferences.h

To understand how AI is changing Agile, let's start with a quick look at how AI has evolved.

The idea of AI isn't new. Scientists have been dreaming of creating "thinking machines" for decades. Early AI programs could do things like play chess or solve simple math problems. However, they were often limited to very specific tasks.

Then came the "Rise of Machine Learning." In recent years, AI has made huge leaps, thanks to "machine learning." Instead of programming a computer with strict rules, we can now feed it tons of data and let it learn patterns on its own. This has led to an avatar of

AI that can recognize images, understand speech, and even generate text.

Imagine an Agile team as a race team. The team needs to communicate clearly, adapt to changing track conditions, and constantly improve their performance.

AI tools are like new high-tech equipment that can help the team. But just having the equipment isn't enough. The team needs to learn how to use it effectively to get the most out of it. That's where Prompt Engineering comes in.

AI and Agile

AI-powered collaboration tools are enhancing the way Agile teams work together. These tools provide real-time language translation, meeting notes summarization, and contextual suggestions during meetings. For example, Slack has integrated AI to facilitate better communication among distributed Agile teams by providing instant translations and summarizing discussions.

Another example is the **Agile Release Train Coach Assistant** and **Scrum Team Assistant Tool** developed by GitHub. These tools assist teams in managing their Agile Release Trains and Scrum practices by offering timely insights and recommendations, thereby improving overall team performance.

Several organizations have successfully integrated AI into their Agile frameworks, demonstrating the transformative potential of this collaboration:

A London-based tech company, Lightful formed a cross-functional "AI Squad" with designers, engineers, and product managers working in daily iterations. They identified specific pain points for their nonprofit clients and experimented with AI solutions in short, rapid cycles. Their most successful innovation was an "AI Feedback" tool that helps nonprofit users improve social media posts by providing suggestions with explanations.

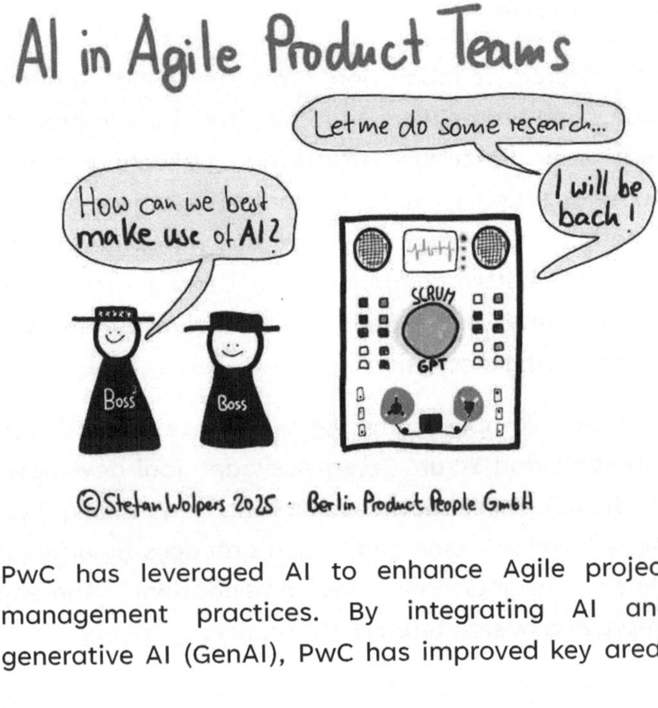

PwC has leveraged AI to enhance Agile project management practices. By integrating AI and generative AI (GenAI), PwC has improved key areas such as refining user stories, predicting workflow bottlenecks, and providing actionable insights from large data sets. This integration has resulted in more effective and efficient Agile practices, driving innovation and focus.

Understanding Prompts and Prompt Engineering

What is a Prompt?

prompt: The ONLY language that AI understands.

In simple terms, *a "prompt" is the input we give to an AI model to tell it what we want it to do.* It's the starting point for the AI's response.

Be it a question: "What are the key features of this product?"

Be it an instruction: "Summarize this user feedback."

It might as well be the beginning of a piece of text: "Write a story about..."

Think of a prompt as a "seed" you plant in the AI's "mind." The quality of the seed and how you plant it greatly influences what grows!

Why Prompt Engineering Matters in Agile

Prompt Engineering is the skill of designing effective prompts to get the best possible results from AI.

Why does it matter? LLMs are powerful, but they're also sensitive to how you ask them things. A poorly worded prompt can lead to:

*i. **Inaccurate information***
*ii. **Irrelevant responses***
*iii. **Wasted time and effort.***

In Agile, this is crucial. Agile teams need to be efficient and avoid rework. Effective Prompt Engineering helps us communicate our needs to AI clearly, ensuring we get valuable outputs quickly.

Imagine you're asking a chef to cook a meal.

A vague request like "Make something delicious" is like a bad prompt. You might get something you don't like!

A detailed request like "Make a spicy Thai green curry with chicken and extra vegetables, and please don't use cilantro" is like a well-engineered prompt. You're much more *likely* to get what you want.

Here, it's important to notice that there would always be scope for refinement of a prompt, no matter what the current output by the engine is.

Prompt Engineering as an Iterative Process

Prompt Engineering is rarely perfect on the first try. It's an iterative process, much like the Agile development process itself.

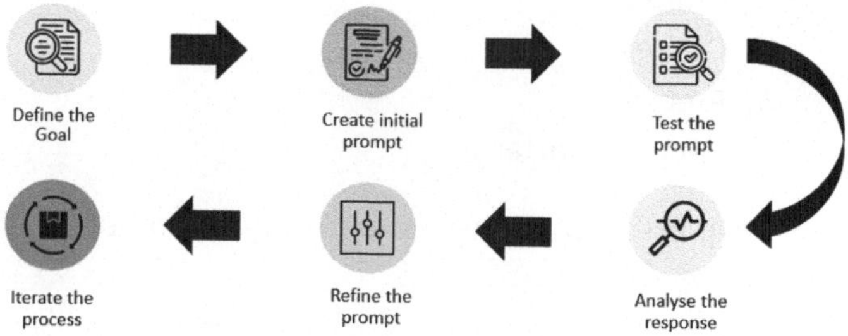

Initial Prompt (Defining a Goal and drafting an initial content request): Our best guess for the desired content.

AI Output (Test the prompt and analyze the Response): Check the correctness of our best guess and analyze what AI does to it.

Evaluation & Refinement (Refine our 'best guess' and repeat. Iterate as many times as needed): We analyze the output, identify what's wrong or missing, and tweak the prompt.

This iterative loop aligns perfectly with the emphasis on continuous improvement and feedback that comes from a truly Agile mindset.

Four Dimensions of Effective Prompts

What makes a prompt "good"? After a lot of research and countless iterations I have discovered the four essential dimensions of Prompting:

1. Clarity
2. Context
3. Precision
4. Persona Pattern

Let's explore each of these prompting techniques with Examples:

CLARITY

Imagine you teaching a new language to a 10-year-old kid. Can you start with complex words and phrases? I think not. We try to keep the grammar and syntax as simple as possible. This ensures that is no ambiguity and things are not left to assumptions while generating the output by the engines.

It is important to understand that clarity of prompt is not a function of length of the prompt. Here are some Examples:

#1

Unclear: "Write a product description."

Clear: "Write a concise and engaging product description for a noise-cancelling headphone, highlighting its battery life, sound quality, and comfort."

#2

Unclear: "Discuss culinary processes that take place on foliaceous stipules of plants with the help of sunlight. Also, mention a green thing and how light, air, and water are important for the aerial parts of the plant.

Clear: "Explain the process of photosynthesis in plants, detailing the role of chlorophyll and how sunlight, carbon dioxide, and water contribute to this biological function."

CONTEXT

How do we humans relate to a conversation and find out what to say next? The answer is 'We have the context'. Similarly, providing a context to AI engines help give the needed information on what are the elements that the engine should relate or think of from its pretrained database to respond to our prompt.

Here are some Examples:

#1

Lack of Context: "Write what happened during the outbreak of the revolutionary war in 1775."

Clear Context: "Describe the historical events leading to the American Revolutionary War, focusing on key incidents like Boston tea party, battle of Saratoga etc. Highlight the tensions between the American and British government and explain how these led to the Revolutionary War in 1775."

#2

Lack of Context: "Write a user story for an application check-out."

Clear Context: "Write a user story for an e-commerce website where a customer can add items to their shopping cart and proceed to check-out."

PRECISION

Imagine a teacher asking a question to a student about a chapter. Would the teacher just mention "Answer something from Chapter 5" or would the teacher be more precise to the exact topic that needs to be answered by the student?

Adding precision helps the AI engine to apply filtration criteria to its database and come up with an output that is only related to the exact direction the question is intended at. Here are some Examples:

Lack of Precision: "Talk about supply and demand and how it is affected in economics."

Precise: "Explain the concept of supply and demand in economics. Describe how an increase in demand can influence pricing with the help of an illustrative example, like the smartphone market."

Lack of Precision: "Give me some data about education industry in India".

Precise: "Explain how digitization is changing the education industry in India, with focus on ed-tech companies and their student-focused strategies"

PERSONA PATTERN

Go back to UX Design and Design Thinking and think about the application and importance of having a persona. It guides the person creating a solution to try and wear the user's boots and think about what the user might think, feel and do.

Providing a persona to AI engines are similar to this. However, this does not make them think but would surely refine the output by focused database search for a particular persona. The prompts with good persona pattern incorporated in them can actually help to humanify the output as it includes specifics to the user.

Here are some Examples:

#1

Lacking Persona: "Write a log entry describing the strange flora and fauna of an uncharted alien planet."

Persona provided: "Pretend you are an astronaut who has just landed on an uncharted alien planet. Write a log entry describing the strange flora and fauna you have encountered, like the colour of the sky and the unfamiliar sounds echoing through the alien landscape. Express your feelings of excitement, curiosity and a hint of apprehension as you document the journey."

#2

Lacking Persona: "Describe the Age of Steam Engines, covering how this led to industrial age"

Persona provided: "Imagine that you are a history teacher teaching grade 5 students. How would you explain the Age of Steam Engines to the children in the class so that they can relate to the invent of engines and how this led to the industrial age, particularly the steel age."

LLM Output Configuration (Brief Overview)

LLM stands for Large Language Model. It's a type of artificial intelligence that can understand and generate human language. These models are trained on vast amounts of text data, allowing them to learn patterns, meanings, and structures of language. They can then use this knowledge to perform tasks like answering questions, writing essays, translating languages, and even creating poetry.

Imagine you have a friend who has read thousands of books, articles, and conversations. This friend has an incredible memory and can recall information from all those readings. When you ask them a question, they can provide a detailed answer based on everything they've learned. They can also help you write a story or translate a sentence into another language because they've seen so many examples of how language works.

An LLM is like this super knowledgeable friend. It has "read" a huge amount of text from the internet, books, and other sources. When you interact with it, it uses its vast knowledge to understand your request and generate a response that makes sense.

LLMs have settings that allow us to control the style and nature of their output. The most common ones are:

Output Length: This determines how many "tokens" (roughly, words or parts of words) the AI will generate.

If you ask for a summary, you'll want a shorter output length.

If you're asking the AI to write a long article, you'll need a longer output length.

Sampling Controls (Temperature, Top-K, Top-P): These settings control the randomness and creativity of the AI's responses.

Temperature: Imagine this as controlling the AI's "imagination."

A low temperature makes the output more predictable and focused (good for factual tasks).

A high temperature makes the output more creative and varied (good for brainstorming).

Top-K and Top-P: These are two different ways of telling the AI to focus on the most likely words when generating text. They also influence the randomness of the output.

We'll explore these in detail later, but for now, think of them as fine-tuning knobs for the AI's behaviour.

Chapter 2

Core Prompting Techniques

Let's now dives into the fundamental techniques for crafting effective prompts. These techniques are the building blocks for more advanced prompting strategies and will significantly improve your interactions with LLMs in Agile workflows.

In this chapter we would build a solid foundation in core prompting techniques. Mastering these will enable you to effectively communicate with LLMs and leverage their power within your Agile workflows.

Here's how to enhance Agile Workflows with effective prompts:

Improving Collaboration: Clear and specific prompts can help Agile teams communicate more effectively with LLMs, ensuring that the information generated is relevant to their needs. For example, using prompts to gather insights on user stories or to predict potential bottlenecks can enhance team collaboration and decision-making.

Optimizing Project Management: Contextual prompts can provide Agile teams with valuable insights into project management practices. By asking LLMs to analyze historical data and forecast project timelines, teams can plan more effectively and respond to changes swiftly. This optimization leads to more efficient workflows and better resource allocation.

Facilitating Innovation: Open-ended questions and iterative refinement can drive innovation within Agile teams. By exploring various aspects of a topic and continuously improving prompts, teams can uncover new ideas and solutions. This iterative process aligns with Agile principles, fostering a culture of continuous improvement and innovation.

Automating Routine Tasks: Using examples and structured prompts, Agile teams can leverage LLMs to automate routine tasks, such as generating meeting summaries or translating documents. This automation frees up time for team members to focus on more strategic activities, enhancing overall productivity.

As we move to further chapters of this book, we would deep dive into use-cases that would show implementation of these. For now, let's focus on the various scenarios of prompting.

Zero-Shot Prompting in Agile Scenarios

What is Zero-Shot Prompting?

Zero-shot prompting is the simplest form of prompting. You give the LLM a task description, and it attempts to complete the task without any additional examples.

Think of it like asking someone a question without giving them any context or hints. You're relying entirely on their general knowledge.

When to Use Zero-Shot Prompting in Agile:

I. For straightforward tasks where the LLM likely has sufficient general knowledge.
II. When you need a quick and simple answer without investing time in providing examples.

Example 1 (User Story Generation):

Prompt: "Write a user story for a customer being able to reset their password."

This relies on the LLM's general understanding of user stories and password reset processes.

Example 2 (Task Summarization):

Prompt: "Summarize the following Agile daily scrum meeting notes:" [followed by the meeting notes]

This leverages the LLM's ability to understand and summarize text.

Imagine asking a colleague, "What's the capital of France?" You expect them to know the answer without you giving them examples of capitals or countries.

One-Shot and Few-Shot Prompting for Agile Tasks

What are One-Shot and Few-Shot Prompting?

These techniques involve providing examples to the LLM within the prompt to guide its output. One-shot prompting gives a single example, while few-shot prompting provides multiple examples.

This helps the LLM understand the desired format, style, or pattern of the response.

When to Use One/Few-Shot Prompting in Agile?

I. When zero-shot prompting doesn't provide the desired output.
II. When you need the LLM to follow a specific format (e.g., JSON, a table).

For more complex tasks where examples help clarify the expected outcome.

Example (*Formatting User Stories*):

Prompt: "Write user stories in the following format: 'As a [user role], I want to [goal], so that [benefit]'.

Example: 'As a customer, I want to be able to track my order, so that I can know when it will arrive."

"Write a user story for a developer being able to deploy code."

This one-shot example sets the structure for the LLM to follow. Once done, all user stories will be written by the LLM in the structure provided in the example within the prompt.

Example (*Extracting Data to JSON*):

Prompt: "Extract the following information into JSON format:

Example 1: 'Name: John Doe, Age: 30, City: New York'

{'Name': 'John Doe', 'Age': '30', 'City': 'New York'}

Example 2: 'Product: Laptop, Price: $1200, Warranty: 1 year'

{'Product': 'Laptop', 'Price': '1200', 'Warranty': '1 year'}

Extract the following: 'Task: Design Database, Duration: 8 hours, Assignee: Jane Smith'"

Once this prompt is given, the extraction would continue to happen in the format prescribed in the above example by the user.

Zero-shot is like saying, "Do this!" without any demonstration.

One-shot is like saying, "Do this, like this," and showing them once.

Few-shot is like saying, "Do this, like this," and showing them several times to illustrate the pattern.

System, Contextual, and Role Prompting in Agile

What is System, Contextual, and Role Prompting?

These techniques add layers of guidance to the LLM, influencing its behaviour and output.

System Prompting: Sets the overall context and purpose. It's like giving the LLM a general mission. It is like setting the rules of a game before you start playing.

Contextual Prompting: Provides specific information relevant to the current task. It's like giving the LLM specific instructions and the details it needs to answer a specific question.

Role Prompting: Assigns a persona or identity to the LLM. It's like asking the LLM to act as a specific expert. Like asking an actor to play a specific character in a movie.

When to Use System/Contextual/Role Prompting in Agile?

I. To provide overarching instructions (system).
II. To give the LLM the necessary background for a task (contextual).

III. To guide the LLM to generate output in a specific style or from a particular viewpoint (role).

Examples:

Example 1 (System Prompting for Code Generation):

Prompt: "You are a helpful AI code generator. Generate Python code to: [task description]"

This system prompt sets the LLM's role and the desired output format (Python code).

Example 2 (Contextual Prompting for User Story Writing):

Prompt: "Context: We are developing an e-commerce platform. The user is a customer. Write a user story for the customer being able to view their order history."

The context clarifies the domain and user, helping the LLM generate a relevant user story.

Example 3 (Role Prompting for Agile Coach):

Prompt: "You are an experienced Agile coach. Provide feedback on the following Scrum Retrospective meeting notes:" [followed by the notes]

This role prompt instructs the LLM to act as an Agile expert and provide relevant feedback.

Chain of Thought (CoT) Prompting for Iterative Thinking

What is Chain of Thought (CoT) Prompting?

Chain of Thought (CoT) Prompting is a technique that enhances the reasoning ability of LLMs. It encourages the LLM to generate intermediate reasoning steps, breaking down a complex problem into smaller, more manageable parts.

Instead of directly providing an answer, the LLM explains its "thinking process" step-by-step, leading to more accurate and transparent results.

CoT prompting can be effectively combined with few-shot prompting to achieve better outcomes in complex tasks that require reasoning.

Where can CoT Prompting be useful?

I. Breaking Down Complex Tasks for LLMs
   a. CoT is particularly useful in Agile (especially for Scrum Masters) when dealing with intricate problems that require logical deduction or multi-step analysis.
   b. By forcing the LLM to articulate its reasoning, we enable it to tackle challenges that would be difficult to solve with a direct, single-step approach.

II. Enhancing Reasoning in Decision-Making
   a. CoT can improve decision-making by providing insights into the LLM's rationale.
   b. This can help teams understand the AI's suggestions, identify potential flaws in its logic, and increase trust in its output.

Here are some Examples:

Example 1: Agile Task Estimation

Prompt: "An Agile team has 5 user stories to complete in a sprint. Story A is estimated at 8 hours, Story B at 13 hours, Story C at 5 hours, Story D at 16 hours, and Story E at 10 hours. The team has 2 developers working 8 hours a day for 5 days. Can they complete all the stories in the sprint? Show your reasoning."

CoT Output:

```
"Step 1: Calculate the total estimated hours: 8 + 13 + 5 + 16 + 10 = 52 hours.

Step 2: Calculate the total available hours: 2 developers * 8 hours/day * 5 days = 80 hours.

Step 3: Compare total estimated hours with total available hours: 52 hours < 80 hours.

Answer: Yes, the team can complete all the stories in the sprint."
```

This is like showing your work in a math problem. The answer alone might be right or wrong, but the steps reveal how you arrived at it.

Example 2: Identifying Dependencies

Prompt: "In a software project, Task A (design the database) must be completed before Task B (create the API). Task C (design the UI) can be done in parallel with Task A. Task D (test the API) must be done after Task B. Task E (test the UI) must be done after Task C. What is the correct sequence of tasks? Show your reasoning."

CoT Output:

"Step 1: Identify the starting tasks: Task A and Task C can start concurrently.

Step 2: Identify tasks dependent on Task A: Task B depends on Task A.

Step 3: Identify tasks dependent on Task B: Task D depends on Task B.

Step 4: Identify tasks dependent on Task C: Task E depends on Task C.

Answer: The correct sequence is A and C (start) -> B -> D, and C -> E."

This is similar to a detective explaining how they pieced together clues to solve a case.

Example 3: Root Cause Analysis

Prompt: "During a sprint review, a bug was found in the user login functionality. The team needs to perform a root cause analysis. The bug occurred because the input validation was not implemented correctly. The input validation was missed because the developer was unfamiliar with the new validation library. Give the step-wise reason for this?"

CoT Output:

"Step 1: Identify the immediate cause: Incorrect input validation.

Step 2: Identify the contributing cause: Developer's unfamiliarity with the library.

Step 3: Investigate the underlying cause: Lack of training or documentation on the new library.

Answer: The root cause is the lack of training or documentation on the new validation library, which led to the developer missing the input validation implementation."

This is like a doctor diagnosing an illness by examining the symptoms, identifying the immediate cause, and then looking for the underlying factors.

Step-Back Prompting for Agile Strategy

What is Step-Back Prompting?

Step-back prompting is a technique that improves LLM performance by prompting it to first consider a more general question related to the specific task. This "**step back**" allows the LLM to activate relevant background knowledge and reasoning processes before tackling the specific problem.

By considering broader principles, LLMs can generate more accurate and insightful responses.

Where can Step-back prompting be used?

I. Using Abstraction for Better LLM Reasoning
    a. Step-back prompting encourages LLMs to think abstractly and apply their knowledge in more creative ways.
    b. It helps the LLM move beyond surface-level details and focus on the underlying concepts.
II. Applying Step-Back Prompting to Agile Planning
    a. For Agile teams, this technique can be valuable for high-level planning, strategy definition, and problem-solving that requires a broader perspective.
    b. It can help teams avoid getting bogged down in details and make more strategic decisions.

Here are some Examples:

Example 1: Sprint Goal Definition

Prompt: "The team needs to define a sprint goal for the next sprint. The user stories include implementing user authentication, creating a user profile page, and allowing users to reset their passwords. What is a good sprint goal?"

Step-Back Prompt:

"What is the overall purpose of these user stories?"

Step-Back Output:

"The overall purpose is to improve user account management."

Final Prompt:

"Given that the overall purpose is to improve user account management, what is a good sprint goal for the next sprint? The user stories include implementing user authentication, creating a user profile page, and allowing users to reset their passwords."

Final Output:

"Sprint Goal: Enhance user account management by implementing authentication, profile creation, and password reset functionality."

It is like asking "Why are we doing this?" before deciding "What exactly are we going to do?"

Example 2: Release Planning

Prompt: "The product owner is planning the next release. Features under consideration include adding a search bar, implementing user reviews, and integrating with social media. What should be the focus of the next release?"

Step-Back Prompt:

"What are the key priorities for the product at this stage?"

Step-Back Output:

"The key priorities are to increase user engagement and gather user feedback."

Final Prompt:

"Given that the key priorities are to increase user engagement and gather user feedback, what should be the focus of the next release? Features under consideration include: adding a search bar, implementing user reviews, and integrating with social media."

Final Output:

"The focus of the next release should be implementing user reviews, as this directly contributes to gathering user feedback and increasing engagement."

It is like asking "What's most important right now?" before deciding "Which projects should we prioritize?"

Example 3: Resolving a Conflict

Prompt: "Two developers are arguing about which technology to use for a new feature. Developer A wants to use Technology X, while Developer B prefers Technology Y. How should they resolve this conflict?"

Step-Back Prompt:

"What are the key principles for making technology decisions in this team?"

Step-Back Output:

"The key principles are choose the technology that best meets the user needs, is maintainable in the long term, and aligns with the team's skillset."

Final Prompt:

"Given that the key principles are: choose the technology that best meets the user needs, is maintainable in the long term, and aligns with the team's skillset, how should Developer A and Developer B resolve the conflict about which technology to use for the new feature?"

Final Output:

"The developers should evaluate Technology X and Technology Y against the key principles: which technology better meets the user needs, which is more maintainable, and which aligns better with the team's

skillset. They should make a decision based on this evaluation."

It is like referring to the team's values before making a tough decision.

Simply put, Step-back prompting is like thinking of a prompt and breaking it down before actually asking the LLM to produce an output.

Now, that we have seen the various patterns and techniques around prompt creation, let us get into the next level to determine the best practices for Prompt Engineering.

Chapter 3

Prompt Engineering Best Practices

In this chapter we would explore the best practices for prompt engineering within Agile teams, focusing on clarity, effective use of examples, structured output, experimentation, and documentation. These practices are crucial for maximizing the efficiency and effectiveness of LLMs in Agile workflows.

In the modern Agile software development, Large Language Models (LLMs) like GPTs are emerging as powerful collaborators, capable of augmenting various tasks from code generation and documentation to user story refinement and test case creation. However, harnessing the full potential of these models requires a thoughtful and disciplined approach to prompt engineering, especially within the iterative and collaborative nature of Agile teams. This chapter delves into the best practices for prompt engineering in this context, emphasizing clarity, effective use of examples, structured output, experimentation, and documentation. By adhering to these principles, Agile teams can maximize the efficiency and effectiveness of LLMs, seamlessly integrating them into their workflows to drive innovation and accelerate delivery.

Clarity, Simplicity, and Specificity in Agile Prompts

The foundation of effective prompt engineering lies in clarity. Just as clear and concise user stories are paramount in Agile, so too are unambiguous prompts for LLMs. A well-defined prompt leaves minimal room for misinterpretation, guiding the model towards generating the desired output. Ambiguous prompts, on the other hand, can lead to irrelevant, inaccurate, or unpredictable results, wasting valuable time and effort.

In Agile, where quick communication and precise task execution are essential, clarity, simplicity, and specificity in prompts are paramount. As mentioned in Chapter 1, Clarity plays a significant role in quality of the output generated by the LLM. Let us take a closer look at these concepts:

Clarity and Simplicity: Prompts should be easy to understand for both the person writing the prompt and the LLM interpreting it. Avoid complex language and unnecessary information.

Think of Agile user stories. They are designed to be simple and clear so that everyone on the team understands what needs to be done. The same principle applies to prompts.

Example:

Original Prompt: "I am currently in New York, and I would appreciate it if you could provide me with some information on interesting places to visit. I am accompanied by two children who are three years old. Could you recommend suitable destinations for our visit?"

Modified Prompt: "Act as a travel guide for tourists. Describe great places to visit in New York Manhattan with a 3 year old."

Specificity: Be precise about the desired output. Generic prompts can lead to vague or irrelevant responses. The more details you provide, the better the LLM can focus on generating what you need.

In Agile, acceptance criteria for a task are very specific. This helps developers know exactly what "done" looks like. Similarly, specific prompts help LLMs understand the expected output.

Example:

Do: "Generate a 3-paragraph blog post about the top 5 video game consoles. The blog post should be informative and engaging, and it should be written in a conversational style."

Do Not: "Generate a blog post about video game consoles."

Action-Oriented Language: Use verbs that clearly describe the desired action. This helps the LLM understand the task.

Examples: "Act," "Analyze," "Categorize," "Classify," "Compare," "Create," "Describe," "Define," "Evaluate," "Extract," "Find," "Generate," "Identify," "List," "Organize," "Parse," "Predict," "Provide," "Recommend," "Rewrite," "Select," "Summarize," "Translate," and "Write."

Best Practices for Clarity:

1. **Be Specific and Direct**: Clearly state the task you want the LLM to perform. Avoid vague language and get straight to the point.
2. **Define the Role and Persona**: Explicitly instruct the LLM to adopt a specific role or persona. This helps the model understand the context and tailor its response accordingly. For example, you might ask it to act as a "technical writer," a "software architect," or a "user experience designer."
3. **Specify the Desired Format**: Clearly indicate the format you expect for the output. This could include bullet points, numbered lists,

JSON, XML, code snippets in a specific language, or a structured paragraph.

4. **Provide Context and Background**: Offer relevant information that the LLM needs to understand the task. This might include the domain, the target audience, existing constraints, or previous steps in a process.
5. **Use Precise Language**: Choose words carefully to avoid ambiguity. Pay attention to terminology and ensure it aligns with the context of your Agile project.
6. **Break Down Complex Tasks**: For intricate tasks, consider breaking them down into smaller, more manageable prompts. This can lead to more focused and accurate results.
7. **Specify Constraints and Limitations**: Clearly define any limitations or constraints that the LLM should adhere to, such as length limits, specific styles, or technologies to avoid.

Prompting Examples and Outputs Illustrating Clarity:

Scenario 1: Generating a User Story

Poor Prompt (Ambiguous): "Write a user story."

Output (Likely Vague): **`"As a user, I want a feature so that I can achieve something."`**

Good Prompt (Clear): "As a user who wants to track the progress of my tasks on the project board, I want to be able to see the completion status of each task visually, so that I can quickly understand the overall project progress."

Output (Specific and Actionable): **"As a project team member, I want to see a visual indicator of the completion status (e.g., percentage complete, status label) for each task on the project board, so that I can easily understand the progress of individual tasks and the overall sprint."**

The clear prompt specifies the user, their goal, and the desired outcome, leading to a much more relevant and actionable user story.

Scenario 2: Explaining a Technical Concept

Poor Prompt (Ambiguous): "Explain microservices."

Output (Potentially Too Technical or Too Basic): **"Microservices are an architectural style..." (could go in various directions).**

Good Prompt (Clear): "Explain microservices to a product owner with limited technical knowledge. Use analogies and avoid jargon."

Output (Accessible Explanation): **"Imagine a large restaurant where everything is managed by one big kitchen. If one part of the kitchen has a problem (like the oven breaking down), it can slow down the entire restaurant.**

Microservices are like having separate, smaller kitchens for different parts of the restaurant - one for appetizers, one for main courses, one for desserts. If the dessert kitchen has an issue, it doesn't necessarily stop the appetizer or main course kitchens from working. Similarly, in software, microservices break down a large application into smaller, independent services that can be developed, deployed, and scaled independently. This makes the overall system more resilient and easier to manage."

Scenario 3: Generating Code

Poor Prompt (Ambiguous): "Write some Python code."

Output (Unclear What Code is Needed): **```python print("Hello, world!")**

Good Prompt: "Write a Python function that takes a list of numbers as input and returns the average of those numbers."

Output:

```python

def calculate_average(numbers):

"""Calculates the average of a list of numbers.

Args:

```
        numbers: A list of numerical values.

    Returns:

        The average of the numbers in the list, or 0 if the list is empty.

    """

    if not numbers:

        return 0

    return sum(numbers) / len(numbers)


# Example usage

data = [1, 2, 3, 4, 5]

average = calculate_average(data)

print(f"The average of {data} is: {average}")
```

The clear prompt explicitly states the programming language, the function's purpose, its input, and the expected output, resulting in the desired code.

The Power of Demonstration: Leveraging Examples for Precise Guidance

Providing examples within prompts is a powerful technique to guide LLMs towards the desired output.

Relevance, Diversity, and Quality of Examples: Examples should be relevant to the task, diverse enough to cover different scenarios, and of high quality to avoid confusing the LLM.

Edge Cases: When possible, include edge cases in your examples to make the LLM more robust. Edge cases are unusual or unexpected inputs that the LLM should still be able to handle.

In software testing, testers create test cases that include not only typical scenarios but also edge cases to ensure the software is reliable.

Ordering of Examples: While the order of examples generally doesn't matter, it's important to mix up classes in classification tasks to avoid overfitting to a specific order.

When training a machine learning model, data scientists shuffle the training data to prevent the model from learning patterns that are specific to the order of the data.

While clear instructions are crucial, providing examples within your prompts can significantly enhance the LLM's ability to understand and generate the desired output. Examples act as concrete demonstrations of the expected format, style, and content, offering the model a more intuitive understanding of your requirements. This is particularly useful when dealing with complex or nuanced tasks where abstract instructions might fall short.

Best Practices for Effective Use of Examples (Few-Shot Prompting):

i. **Provide Relevant and High-Quality Examples:** The examples you provide should closely resemble the desired output in terms of format, style, and content. Ensure they are accurate and representative of what you're looking for.

ii. **Start with a Few Examples (Few-Shot)**: Often, even a small number of well-chosen examples (2-5) can significantly improve the model's performance. This technique is known as "few-shot prompting."

iii. **Vary the Examples (When Necessary)**: If the desired output can have variations, provide examples that showcase these different possibilities to guide the model accordingly.

iv. **Clearly Separate Instructions from Examples:** Use clear delimiters (e.g., "### Instruction:", "### Examples:", "### Output:") to distinguish between your instructions and the examples.

v. **Ensure Consistency Between Instructions and Examples:** The examples should align with the instructions you've provided. Inconsistencies can confuse the model.

vi. **Iterate on Examples:** If the initial results are not satisfactory, refine your examples and try again. Experiment with different examples to see which ones yield the best results.

Scenario 1: Generating Commit Messages

Prompt: "Write a concise and informative Git commit message based on the following code changes."

```
### Code Changes:
Fixed a bug where the user's profile picture was not updating correctly.

### Commit Message:
Fix: Ensure user profile picture updates correctly
```

```
### Code Changes:
Implemented the user authentication feature using JWT.

### Commit Message:
Feat: Implement user authentication with JWT
```

```
### Code Changes:
Refactored the database query for fetching user data to improve performance.

### Commit Message:
Refactor: Optimize database query for user data
```

Code Changes:

Added unit tests for the user authentication service.

Output:

```
Test: Add unit tests for user authentication service
```

Scenario 2: Extracting Information in a Specific Format

Prompt: "Extract the product name and price from the following text and output them as a JSON object."

Examples:

```
### Text:
The new "SuperGadget X1" is now available for $49.99.

### JSON Output:
{
  "product_name": "SuperGadget X1",
  "price": 49.99
}
```

```
### Text:
Get the "UltraBlender 3000" today for just $129.

### JSON Output:
{
  "product_name": "UltraBlender 3000",
  "price": 129.00
}
```

Text:

Introducing the "SmartWatch Pro" priced at $199.95.

Output:

```json
{
  "product_name": "SmartWatch Pro",
  "price": 199.95
}
```

The examples clearly demonstrate the desired JSON format for the extracted information, enabling the LLM to accurately process the new text.

Scenario 3: Translating Technical Terms with Context

Prompt: "Translate the following English technical terms into Spanish, considering the context of software development."

Output:

```
### English:
Bug

### Spanish:
Error (when referring to a software defect)
```

```
### English:
Feature

### Spanish:
Funcionalidad
```

English: Deployment

Output:

```
Despliegue (in the context of software release)
```

The examples provide context-specific translations, ensuring that the LLM understands the intended meaning of the technical terms within the software development domain.

Structured Output and Data Handling

For tasks that involve extracting, selecting, parsing, or categorizing data, structured output formats like JSON or XML are highly beneficial.

In an Agile environment, where information needs to be easily digestible and integrated into various workflows, requesting structured output from LLMs is crucial. Well-structured output enhances readability, facilitates parsing and automation, and ensures consistency across different generations.

Benefits of JSON:

JSON output can be directly used in applications, eliminating the need for manual parsing.

It helps the LLM create a clear structure, reducing hallucinations and improving the organization of the output, especially with datetime objects.

APIs often return data in JSON format because it's a standard and easy for computers to process. Using JSON in prompts aligns with this practice.

Best Practices for Requesting Structured Output:

i. **Specify the Output Format Explicitly**: Clearly state the desired output format (e.g., JSON, XML, CSV, Markdown, bullet points, numbered lists, tables).

ii. **Define the Structure and Schema**: If you need a specific structure (e.g., a JSON object with particular keys and value types), provide a clear definition or even a template.

iii. **Use Delimiters for Clarity**: Employ clear delimiters (e.g., json ... for JSON, xml ... for XML, or specific separators for CSV) to make the output easily identifiable and parsable.

iv. **Request Consistent Formatting**: Ask the LLM to maintain consistent formatting throughout the output (e.g., capitalization, indentation, use of quotes).

v. **Provide Examples of the Desired Structure**: As seen in the previous section, examples are highly effective in demonstrating the desired output structure.

vi. **Iterate on the Structure**: If the initial output structure is not ideal, refine your prompt and provide feedback to guide the LLM towards the desired format.

Working with Schemas: Providing a schema to the LLM can further guide the output structure and the data types within it.

Example: Providing a schema for movie reviews, specifying the fields "sentiment" (with allowed values) and "name," ensures that the LLM returns the data in the desired format.

In database design, a schema defines how data is organized. Providing a schema to an LLM is like giving it a blueprint for the output.

JSON Repair: LLMs can be prompted to repair invalid JSON outputs, ensuring that the data is usable.

This is particularly useful in real-world applications where LLM outputs might occasionally have errors.

Scenario 1: Generating a List of Acceptance Criteria

Prompt: "Generate a list of acceptance criteria for the user story: 'As a user, I want to be able to filter the product catalogue by price range.'"

Desired Output Format: Bulleted list.

```
* The user should be able to specify a minimum price.
* The user should be able to specify a maximum price.
* The system should display only products within the specified price range.
* The system should handle cases where the minimum price is greater than the maxim
* The filtering should be applied in real-time or with a clear "Apply" button.
* The price range input fields should accept numerical values only.
```

By requesting a bulleted list, the prompt ensures that the acceptance criteria are presented in a clear and easily readable format.

Scenario 2: Generating Test Cases in a Table Format

Prompt: "Generate three test cases for the login functionality. Include columns for 'Test Case ID', 'Test Description', 'Input', and 'Expected Output'."

Desired Output Format: Markdown table.

Output:

Markdown

```
| Test Case ID | Test Description | Input | Expected Output |
|--------------|---------------------------|---------------------------|-----------------------------------------------|
| TC_LOGIN_001 | Successful login | Valid username and password | User is successfully logged in and redirected to the dashboard. |
| TC_LOGIN_002 | Incorrect password | Valid username, invalid password | Error message "Invalid username or password" is displayed. |
| TC_LOGIN_003 | Empty username and password | Empty username, empty password | Error messages are displayed for both empty fields. |
```

Experimentation, Iteration, and Adaptation

Prompt engineering is not a one-time activity but rather an iterative process of experimentation and refinement. The initial prompt may not always yield the desired results, and Agile teams should embrace a mindset of continuous improvement, treating prompt engineering as an ongoing learning experience.

Experimentation: Try different models, model configurations, prompt formats, word choices, and styles to see how they affect the output.

Agile development involves experimentation. Teams try different approaches, measure the results, and adapt their process. Prompt engineering follows a similar pattern.

Iterative Refinement: Refine your prompts based on the LLM's output. Adjust the prompt until it consistently produces the desired results.

Control the length of the LLM's response either through the model's configuration or by explicitly requesting a specific length in the prompt.

Adaptation to Model Updates: Stay informed about updates to LLM architectures, training data, and capabilities, and adjust your prompts to leverage new features and maintain effectiveness.

In Agile, teams continuously adapt to changing requirements and feedback. Prompt engineering also requires adapting to the evolving capabilities of LLMs.

Best Practices for Experimentation and Refinement:

i. **Start Simple and Iterate**: Begin with a straightforward prompt and gradually add complexity or refine the instructions based on the model's output.
ii. **Vary Prompt Components**: Experiment with different phrasing, keywords, instructions, examples, and output formats to see what works best for a given task.
iii. **Test Different Models (If Applicable)**: If your platform allows, experiment with different

LLM models, as they may have varying strengths and weaknesses.

iv. **Analyze the Output Critically**: Carefully evaluate the LLM's output, identifying what works well and what needs improvement.

v. **Provide Feedback to the Model (If Possible)**: Some platforms allow you to provide feedback (e.g., thumbs up/down) on the generated output, which can help the model learn over time.

vi. **Keep Track of Your Experiments**: Document the prompts you've tried, the corresponding outputs, and your observations. This helps you identify patterns and learn from your successes and failures.

vii. **Collaborate and Share Learnings**: Within the Agile team, encourage collaboration on prompt engineering. Share successful prompts and insights to build collective knowledge.

Scenario: Summarizing User Feedback

Initial Prompt (Simple): "Summarize the following user feedback."

User Feedback: "The navigation is confusing. I can't find the settings page. Also, the loading times are too slow. The design looks nice, though."

Initial Output (Generic): **"Users find the navigation confusing and experience slow loading times. They also like the design."**

Refined Prompt (Adding Specificity): "Summarize the following user feedback, categorizing the feedback into 'Positive' and 'Negative' aspects."

Refined Output (Categorized):

```
Negative:
- Confusing navigation
- Difficulty finding the settings page
- Slow loading times

Positive:
- Nice design
```

Further Refined Prompt (Requesting Actionable Insights): "Summarize the following user feedback and suggest potential areas for improvement based on the negative feedback."

Further Refined Output (Actionable Insights):

```
Summary: Users find the navigation confusing and experience slow loading time, but appreciate the design.

Potential Areas for Improvement:
– Navigation: Re-evaluate the information architecture and user flow to make navigation more intuitive. Consider user testing to identify pain points.
– Performance: Investigate the causes of slow loading times and implement optimizations.
```

Scenario: Generating Different Styles of Documentation

Initial Prompt: "Write documentation for the user authentication feature."

Initial Output (Potentially Too Technical): "The user authentication module utilizes JWT

for secure token-based authentication. Upon successful login, a JWT is issued..."

Refined Prompt (Targeting a Specific Audience): "Write user-friendly documentation for the user authentication feature, explaining how new users can create an account and how existing users can log in."

Refined Output (User-Friendly):

```
Creating an Account:
1. Go to the registration page.
2. Fill in the required fields (username, email, password).
3. Click the "Register" button.
4. You will receive a confirmation email. Click the link in the email to activate :

Logging In:
1. Go to the login page.
2. Enter your registered username and password.
3. Click the "Login" button.
4. You will be redirected to your dashboard.
```

This example demonstrates how iteratively refining the prompt by adding specific instructions and desired output structures can lead to more insightful and actionable results.

Documenting and Sharing Prompts Within the Agile Team

Documenting and sharing prompts are crucial for collaboration, consistency, and knowledge sharing within Agile teams. This not only ensures some level of consistency in the outcomes but also let's the users (agile team) to curate ways to look at these further.

Prompt Tables: Using a structured format like tables to document prompts helps in organizing information like the goal, model, configuration, and examples.

This is particularly important as prompts often go through many iterations.

Agile teams use tools like Jira or Trello to track tasks and progress. Prompt tables serve a similar purpose for prompt engineering.

Example:

Field	Value
Goal	Generate user stories for a new feature
Model	`gemini-pro`
Temperature	0.8
Top-K	40
Top-P	0.95
Prompt	"As a [User Role], I want to [Goal], so that [Benefit]"
Output	A list of user stories in the specified format.
Notes	Add context about the feature for more relevant user stories.

Field	Value
Goal	Summarize user feedback from a survey
Model	`gemini-pro`
Temperature	0.7
Top-K	30
Top-P	0.9
Prompt	"Summarize the following user feedback, highlighting key pain points and suggestions for improvement: [User Feedback Data]"
Output	A concise summary with bullet points of pain points and improvement suggestions.
Notes	Use temperature 0.5 for more factual summary.

Variables in Prompts: Using variables in prompts makes them more dynamic and reusable. Instead of hardcoding values, variables can be used and changed for different inputs.

Example: A prompt that provides facts about a city can use a variable for the city name, allowing the prompt to be used for different cities.

In programming, variables are used to store data that can change. This makes the code more flexible and reusable.

Prompt Libraries: Create a shared repository or library of effective prompts that the team can use and contribute to. This avoids duplication of effort and ensures consistency.

Agile teams often have shared code repositories or design pattern libraries. A prompt library serves a similar purpose for prompt engineering.

Collaboration: Encourage team members to experiment with prompts together and share their findings. This can lead to new insights and more effective prompts.

Agile emphasizes collaboration and knowledge sharing. Pair programming or code reviews are examples of this. Collaborative prompt engineering aligns with these principles.

As we conclude this chapter, remember that prompt engineering is a dynamic and rapidly evolving field, much like Agile itself. The principles and practices outlined here provide a strong foundation, but the journey doesn't end here. The future holds even more sophisticated prompting techniques, advanced LLM capabilities, and innovative ways for Agile teams to collaborate with AI. By staying curious, continuously learning, and actively participating in the prompt engineering community, you'll not only master the current state-of-the-art but also shape the future of Agile-AI collaboration.

The next chapter will build on this foundation by exploring advanced prompting techniques.

Part 2

Role Specific Prompt Engineering

Chapter 4

Prompt Engineering for Scrum Masters

This chapter explores the transformative potential of prompt engineering for Scrum Masters and how strategically crafted prompts can amplify a Scrum Master's ability to facilitate events with greater precision, foster stronger team collaboration, streamline communication with stakeholders, and even automate traditionally time-consuming administrative tasks. From helping the team generate user stories that resonate with clarity to extracting actionable insights from retrospective feedback, the power of AI, guided by effective prompts, is poised to redefine the very role of the Scrum Master.

The role of the Scrum Master, traditionally focused on facilitating Agile processes, coaching the team, and removing impediments, is undergoing a significant transformation in the wake of Artificial Intelligence, particularly Generative AI. This chapter explores the evolving landscape of the Scrum Master role, tracing its historical trajectory in relation to AI adoption and highlighting how Scrum Masters globally are increasingly leveraging prompt engineering as a crucial skill to enhance their effectiveness. We will delve into real-world examples across diverse domains, showcasing the positive impact of prompt engineering on various Scrum Master responsibilities.

Scrum Masters and the Dawn of AI

The Scrum framework, since its formalization in the early 1990s, has emphasized human collaboration, self-organization, and continuous improvement. The Scrum Master's role emerged as a servant-leader, guiding the team towards these principles. Initially, the focus was heavily on process adherence, facilitating Scrum events (Sprint Planning, Daily Scrum, Sprint Review, Sprint Retrospective), and coaching the team on Agile values and practices.

As AI began to permeate various industries, it's potential impact on software development and Agile methodologies became apparent. Early AI applications in development often focused on automation of repetitive tasks like testing or code analysis.

However, the advent of Generative AI, with its ability to understand and generate human-like text, code, and other media, has introduced a paradigm shift.

Initially, there might have been some apprehension about AI potentially replacing human roles within Agile teams, including the Scrum Master. Questions arose about whether AI could facilitate ceremonies, track progress, or even coach teams. However, the reality has proven to be far more nuanced and collaborative. Instead of replacement, the focus has shifted towards augmentation – how AI, powered by effective prompt engineering, can empower Scrum Masters to be even more effective in their roles.

The Evolving Role: From Facilitator to AI-Augmented Coach

The integration of Generative AI is not diminishing the importance of the Scrum Master; rather, it is augmenting their capabilities and allowing them to focus on higher-value activities. The core responsibilities of a Scrum Master – fostering a high-performing team, ensuring a smooth workflow, and promoting continuous improvement – remain critical. However, AI tools, driven by well-crafted prompts, can assist in various aspects of these responsibilities:

i. **Enhanced Facilitation**: AI can help prepare for and summarize Scrum events, identify key discussion points, and even analyze team sentiment during retrospectives.
ii. **Improved Impediment Removal**: AI can assist in identifying potential impediments by analyzing team communication and project data, and even suggest potential solutions based on vast knowledge bases.

iii. **More Effective Coaching**: AI can provide personalized coaching insights based on team dynamics and individual performance patterns, allowing Scrum Masters to tailor their guidance.
iv. **Streamlined Reporting and Documentation**: AI can automate the generation of sprint reports, meeting minutes, and other documentation, freeing up the Scrum Master's time.
v. **Proactive Risk Management**: AI can analyze project data to identify potential risks and proactively alert the Scrum Master.

The key to unlocking this potential lies in the Scrum Master's ability to effectively communicate with these AI tools through skilful prompt engineering.

The Rise of Prompt Engineering for Scrum Masters

Prompt engineering, the art and science of crafting effective prompts that elicit desired responses from LLMs, is becoming an indispensable skill for modern Scrum Masters. Just as a skilled facilitator knows how to ask the right questions to guide a team, an AI-savvy Scrum Master knows how to formulate prompts that extract valuable insights and generate helpful outputs from AI tools.

What is the Big Deal about Prompt Engineering for Scrum Masters?

i. **Maximizing the Value of AI Tools**: Without well-crafted prompts, the output from AI tools can be generic, irrelevant, or even misleading. Effective prompts ensure that the AI provides specific, actionable information tailored to the Scrum Master's needs.

ii. **Tailoring AI Assistance**: Prompt engineering allows Scrum Masters to customize the AI's role, tone, and output format to suit different situations and team dynamics.

iii. **Unlocking Deeper Insights**: Skilful prompting can help uncover hidden patterns, identify subtle issues, and generate creative solutions that might not be immediately apparent.

iv. **Saving Time and Effort**: By effectively guiding AI tools, Scrum Masters can automate tasks and access information more quickly, freeing up time for more strategic and people-centric activities.

v. **Improving Communication and Collaboration**: AI-generated summaries, reports, and insights, driven by clear prompts, can enhance communication within the team and with stakeholders.

Global Leverage: Real Positive Examples Across Domains

Scrum Masters across various industries are already experimenting with and benefiting from prompt engineering in their daily work. Here are some real positive examples, categorized by common Scrum Master responsibilities:

Enhancing Sprint Planning:

Scenario: A Scrum Master in an e-commerce company is facilitating Sprint Planning for a team working on improving the checkout process.

Prompt Example: "Act as a user experience expert. Based on the following user stories for the checkout process [list of user stories], identify potential edge cases and user pain points that the team should consider during planning. Output as a bulleted list of questions."

Outcome: **The AI, acting as a UX expert, generated insightful questions about error handling, payment gateway integration issues, and mobile responsiveness, prompting the team to proactively address these potential challenges during the sprint planning, leading to a smoother development process and a more robust feature.**

Scenario: A Scrum Master in a healthcare software company is helping the team estimate the effort for new features in their patient portal.

Prompt Example: "Analyze the following user stories [list of user stories] and, considering the team's past velocity of [average velocity], provide a rough estimate in story points for each story, along with a brief justification based on potential technical complexity and dependencies. Output as a table with columns 'User Story', 'Estimated Points', and 'Justification'."

Positive Outcome: **The AI provided initial estimates with clear justifications, helping the team have a more informed discussion about effort and capacity during planning, leading to more realistic sprint commitments.**

Facilitating More Effective Daily Scrums:

Scenario: A Scrum Master in a fintech company wants to ensure the Daily Scrum remains focused and efficient.

Prompt Example: "Act as a Daily Scrum facilitator. Based on the team's updates from the last Daily Scrum [provide the transcript or summary], identify any potential blockers or dependencies that were mentioned but not fully addressed. Output as a bulleted list of follow-up questions for specific team members."

Positive Outcome: **The AI identified a lingering dependency between two developers that hadn't been explicitly addressed. The Scrum Master used the AI's output to ask targeted follow-up questions, leading to a clearer plan for resolving the dependency and preventing potential delays.**

Scenario: A Scrum Master for a team developing a video streaming platform wants to gauge team sentiment during the Daily Scrum.

Prompt Example: "Analyze the following transcript of the Daily Scrum [provide the transcript]. Identify the overall sentiment of the team (positive, neutral, or negative) and highlight any phrases or keywords that indicate potential frustration or uncertainty. Output a brief summary of the sentiment and a list of supporting quotes."

Positive Outcome: **The AI identified a slightly negative sentiment related to a particular technical challenge. The Scrum Master used this insight to proactively schedule a follow-up discussion to address the team's concerns and offer support.**

Revolutionizing Sprint Retrospectives:

Scenario: A Scrum Master in a SaaS company wants to gather more insightful feedback during the Sprint Retrospective.

Prompt Example: "Based on the events and challenges faced during the last sprint [provide a brief summary], brainstorm three creative and thought-provoking questions that can encourage the team to reflect on what went well, what could be improved, and what new ideas they have for the next sprint. Avoid generic questions like 'What went well?'"

Outcome: **The AI generated questions like, "If our last sprint was a weather pattern, what would it be and why?", "What's one 'hidden gem' of our process that we should celebrate and amplify?", and "What's one assumption we made this sprint that we should challenge next time?". These prompts led to a more engaging and insightful retrospective, uncovering deeper issues and generating more innovative improvement ideas.**

Scenario: A Scrum Master in a manufacturing company wants to analyze past retrospective data to identify recurring themes.

Prompt Example: "Analyze the transcripts from the last five Sprint Retrospectives [provide the transcripts]. Identify the top three recurring themes related to team challenges and suggest potential overarching action items that could address these themes. Output as a numbered list of themes with corresponding suggested action items."

Outcome: **The AI identified recurring issues related to communication silos and inconsistent testing. The Scrum Master used this analysis to propose team-wide initiatives focused on improving cross-team communication and standardizing testing practices.**

Streamlining Impediment Removal:

Scenario: A Scrum Master in a logistics company is facing a recurring impediment related to integration with a legacy system.

Prompt Example: "Describe the following technical impediment in detail [provide a detailed description of the integration issue]. Based on your knowledge of common integration challenges and potential solutions, suggest three possible approaches to mitigate this impediment, along with potential risks and benefits for each approach. Output as a table with columns 'Proposed Solution', 'Potential Benefits', and 'Potential Risks'."

Positive Outcome: **The AI provided three distinct approaches to address the integration issue, outlining the pros and cons of each. This helped the Scrum Master present a well-informed set of options to**

the development team and stakeholders, leading to a more efficient resolution.

Scenario: A Scrum Master for a team developing an online learning platform is dealing with team members feeling overwhelmed by the workload.

Prompt Example: "Analyze the following team feedback from the Daily Scrums and informal conversations [provide a summary of the feedback]. Identify potential underlying causes for the team feeling overwhelmed and suggest three actionable strategies the Scrum Master could implement to address this issue, focusing on workload management and team well-being. Output as a numbered list of strategies with a brief explanation for each."

Outcome: **The AI suggested strategies such as visualizing workload distribution, implementing WIP limits, and facilitating a discussion on task prioritization. The Scrum Master implemented these strategies, leading to a more balanced workload and improved team morale.**

Enhancing Coaching and Team Development:

Scenario: A Scrum Master for a game development team wants to provide personalized coaching to a junior developer struggling with test-driven development (TDD).

Prompt Example: "Act as an experienced software development mentor. Based on the following code snippet written by a junior developer [provide the code] and their stated difficulty with writing unit tests first, provide three specific and actionable tips on how they can approach TDD for this particular piece of code. Focus on small, incremental steps and clear examples."

Outcome: **The AI provided targeted advice with specific examples related to the developer's code, helping the Scrum Master offer more effective and practical guidance, leading to the junior developer's improved understanding and adoption of TDD.**

Scenario: A Scrum Master working with a volunteer team wants to foster better collaboration and communication within the team.

Prompt Example: "Based on the following observations of team interactions during the last sprint [provide a summary of observations], suggest three icebreaker activities or team-building exercises that could help improve communication and collaboration within this volunteer team, considering their diverse backgrounds and limited availability for extra meetings. Provide brief instructions for each activity."

Outcome: **The AI suggested quick and engaging activities that could be incorporated into existing meetings, leading to improved team bonding and more effective communication.**

Automating Reporting and Documentation:

Scenario: A Scrum Master in a telecom company needs to generate a weekly sprint report for stakeholders.

Prompt Example: "Based on the following data from our project management tool [provide the data in a structured format], generate a concise weekly sprint report that includes: a summary of completed user stories, any blockers encountered and their resolution status, the team's velocity for the week, and any key learnings or observations. Format the report using Markdown headings and bullet points."

Outcome: **The AI automated the generation of the sprint report, saving the Scrum Master significant time and ensuring consistent reporting to stakeholders.**

Scenario: A Scrum Master wants to quickly summarize the key discussion points from a Sprint Review meeting.

Prompt Example: "Analyze the following transcript of the Sprint Review meeting [provide the transcript]. Identify the key features demonstrated, the feedback received from stakeholders, and any action items agreed upon. Output a summary with clear headings for each of these categories."

Outcome: **The AI generated a concise summary of the Sprint Review, making it easy for the Scrum Master to share the key takeaways and action items with the team and stakeholders.**

Thriving on Prompt Engineering: The Future of the AI-Augmented Scrum Master

The examples above illustrate the immense potential of prompt engineering for Scrum Masters across various domains. As AI tools become more sophisticated and integrated into Agile workflows, the ability to craft effective prompts will become an even more critical differentiator for highly effective Scrum Masters.

Now, let us see some examples and use cases that represent the current frontier of AI-assisted Scrum Mastery. As LLMs continue to evolve, and as our understanding of prompt engineering deepens, the possibilities will expand exponentially.

Enhancing Agile Events with Prompts (specifically Scrum)

Events of Scrum are crucial for Agile teams to plan, execute, review, inspect and adapt their work. Prompt engineering can significantly enhance the value and efficiency of these events. Let's explore some of these contents.

Sprint Planning: Generating User Stories and Acceptance Criteria

Scrum Masters can use prompts to assist the team in the creation of well-formed user stories and clear acceptance criteria during or before the Sprint Planning event. This ensures that the developers have a clear understanding of what needs to be built and how it will be validated.

Examples:

Prompt: "As a [User Role], I want to [Goal], so that [Benefit]. Generate 3 user stories for an e-commerce website feature that allows users to filter products by price."

Output:

"As a customer, I want to filter products by price range, so that I can find products that fit my budget."

"As a customer, I want to sort products by price (ascending and descending), so that I can easily find the cheapest or most expensive products."

"As a customer, I want to see the price range clearly displayed, so that I understand the minimum and maximum price of the products displayed"

Prompt: "For the user story 'As a customer, I want to filter products by colour, so that I can quickly find products in my preferred colour,' write 5 detailed acceptance criteria."

Output:

"Verify that the user can select one or more colours from a predefined list."

"Verify that the product list is updated to show only products that match the selected colour(s)."

"Verify that the number of products matching the selected colour(s) is displayed."

"Verify that the user can clear the colour filter to view all products."

"Verify that the colour filter works correctly in combination with other filters (e.g., price, size)."

Daily Scrum: Summarizing Discussions and Identifying Blockers

Prompts can help Scrum Masters quickly summarize the key points of the Daily Scrum and identify any impediments that need to be addressed. This ensures that everyone is on the same page and that blockers are resolved promptly.

Examples:

Prompt: "Summarize the following Daily Scrum discussion: [*Daily Scrum Transcript*]"

Output: **"Key points: John is working on the user authentication feature and is facing a blocker with the API integration. Sarah completed the product page design. David is testing the user registration flow. Blockers: API integration issue."**

Prompt: "Identify any potential blockers in the following Daily Scrum: [*Daily Scrum*]"

Output: **"Potential blockers: John is waiting for the API to be ready. Mary needs design feedback before proceeding with the implementation."**

Sprint Review/ System Demo: Creating Compelling Presentations and Demos

Scrum Masters can use prompts to create engaging presentations and demos that showcase the team's accomplishments during the sprint. This helps to effectively communicate the value delivered to stakeholders.

Examples:

Prompt: "Create a visually appealing presentation outline for a Sprint Review showcasing the following features: user login, product catalogue, shopping cart."

Output:

"Slide 1: Sprint Goal"

"Slide 2: User Login Demo"

"Slide 3: Product Catalogue Overview"

"Slide 4: Shopping Cart Functionality Demo"

"Slide 5: Key Metrics and Achievements"

Prompt: "Write a concise and persuasive script for a demo of the user login feature."

Output: **"In this demo, we'll show you how users can easily and securely log in to the application. We've implemented a streamlined login process with enhanced security measures to protect user data."**

Sprint Retrospective: Analyzing Feedback and Suggesting Improvements

Prompts can assist in analyzing feedback from the Sprint Retrospective and generating actionable suggestions for improvement. This helps the team to continuously learn and adapt its processes.

Examples:

Prompt: "Analyze the following Sprint Retrospective feedback and identify the top 3 areas for improvement: [*Retrospective Feedback*]"

Output: **"Top 3 areas for improvement: 1. Improve communication between the development and testing teams. 2. Refine the estimation process to increase accuracy. 3. Reduce the number of interruptions during the sprint."**

Prompt: "Suggest specific actions to improve communication between the development and testing teams, based on the following feedback: 'The testing team often receives features late in the sprint, leading to rushed testing and potential bugs.'"

Output:

"Implement a 'Definition of Ready' to ensure that user stories are fully defined before development begins."

"Conduct regular meetings between developers and testers to discuss progress and potential issues."

"Use a shared communication channel to provide real-time updates on feature development."

Facilitating Team Collaboration with AI Prompts

Prompt engineering can also help Scrum Masters foster a more collaborative and productive team environment.

Conflict Resolution and Mediation: Scrum Masters can use prompts to get objective perspectives on conflicts and generate potential solutions. This can help to facilitate constructive dialogue and find mutually agreeable resolutions.

Examples:

Prompt: "Two developers are in disagreement about the best approach to implement a feature. Developer A wants to use Technology X, while Developer B prefers Technology Y. What are the pros and cons of each technology, and what are some possible ways to resolve this conflict?"

Output: **"Pros of Technology X: [List of Pros]. Cons of Technology X: [List of Cons]. Pros of Technology Y: [List of Pros]. Cons of Technology Y: [List of Cons]. Possible solutions: 1. Evaluate both technologies against the project requirements and choose the one that best fits. 2. Use Technology X for one part of the feature and Technology Y for another. 3. Conduct a spike to prototype both technologies and gather more data."**

Prompt: "The product owner and the development team have different expectations about the scope of a user story. How can the Scrum Master facilitate a discussion to align their understanding?"

Output: **"The Scrum Master can: 1. Facilitate a detailed discussion of the user story, focusing on the acceptance criteria. 2. Use visual aids to clarify the scope. 3. Break down the user story into smaller tasks. 4. Refer to the Definition of Done to ensure everyone has a shared understanding of completion."**

Case Study: An Agile consultancy uses LLMs to analyze team communication and identify potential sources of conflict. The LLM provides insights to the Scrum Master, enabling them to proactively address issues and promote a more harmonious team dynamic.

Team Building and Motivation: Scrum Masters can use prompts to generate ideas for team-building activities, icebreakers, and motivational messages. This can help to improve team morale and create a more positive work environment.

Examples:

Prompt: "Suggest 5 fun and engaging team-building activities for a remote Agile team."

Output: **"1. Virtual escape room. 2. Online team trivia. 3. Show and tell. 4. Virtual coffee break. 5. Online Pictionary."**

Prompt: "Write an inspirational message to motivate the team after a challenging sprint."

Output: **"Team, I know this sprint was particularly demanding, and we faced some unexpected hurdles. However, your resilience and dedication shone through, and we still managed to deliver valuable increments. Let's celebrate our achievements and learn from the challenges to come back even stronger next sprint!"**

Knowledge Management and Documentation: Prompts can help Scrum Masters create and maintain team documentation, such as meeting notes, decisions, and action items. This ensures that knowledge is captured and shared effectively.

Examples:

Prompt: "Generate meeting notes from the following discussion: [Meeting Transcript]"

Output: **"Meeting Notes: Topic: Sprint Planning. Decisions: The team committed to completing User Stories 1, 2, and 3. Action Items: John to create the database schema. Sarah to design the user interface."**

Prompt: "Create a FAQ document for new team members, covering the following topics: sprint planning, daily scrum, sprint review, sprint retrospective."

Output: **"FAQ: 1. What is Sprint Planning? [Explanation]. 2. What is the Daily Scrum? [Explanation]. 3. What is the Sprint Review?**

[Explanation]. 4. What is the Sprint Retrospective? [Explanation]"

Improving Communication and Reporting

Effective communication and reporting are essential for keeping stakeholders informed and ensuring transparency. Prompt engineering can help Scrum Masters streamline these processes.

Generating Status Reports and Updates: Scrum Masters can use prompts to quickly generate concise and informative status reports for stakeholders. This saves time and ensures that everyone is aware of the team's progress.

Examples:

Prompt: "Generate a weekly sprint status report, including progress on each user story, any blockers, and the overall sprint progress."

Output: **"Sprint Status Report: User Story 1: In progress. User Story 2: Completed. User Story 3: Blocked due to API issue. Overall Sprint Progress: On track."**

Prompt: "Create a brief email update for stakeholders, highlighting the key achievements of the sprint and any upcoming milestones."

Output: **"Dear Stakeholders, this sprint, we successfully completed the user login feature and the product catalogue. Our next**

milestone is to implement the shopping cart functionality. Thank you for your continued support."

Creating Stakeholder Communications: Prompts can help Scrum Masters draft various types of communication to stakeholders, such as announcements, meeting agendas, and feedback requests. This ensures clear and effective communication.

Examples:

Prompt: "Draft an announcement email to users about the upcoming release of a new feature."

Output: **"Dear Users, We're excited to announce the upcoming release of our new [Feature]! This feature will allow you to [Benefit]. We'll be releasing it on [Date]. Stay tuned for more updates!"**

Prompt: "Create an agenda for a meeting with stakeholders to gather feedback on the user interface design."

Output: **"Meeting Agenda: 1. Introduction (5 minutes). 2. Overview of the UI Design (10 minutes). 3. Feedback on the Homepage (15 minutes). 4. Feedback on the Product Page (15 minutes). 5. Next Steps (5 minutes)."**

Visualizing Data and Progress: Prompts can assist Scrum Masters in generating visualizations of data and progress, such as burndown charts or velocity charts. This helps to communicate the team's performance in a clear and compelling way.

Examples:

Prompt: "Generate a burndown chart based on the following sprint data: [*Sprint Data*]"

Output: (The LLM can describe the chart or provide data that can be used to create the chart) **"The burndown chart shows a steady decrease in the remaining work throughout the sprint, with a slight deviation on Day 3 due to an unexpected blocker. The team is currently on track to complete the sprint on time."**

Prompt: "Create a velocity chart for the past 5 sprints, based on the following data: [*Velocity Data*]"

Output: (The LLM can describe the chart or provide data for the chart) **"The velocity chart shows that the team's velocity has been relatively consistent over the past 5 sprints, with an average velocity of [Number]. There was a slight dip in velocity in Sprint 3 due to team member absence."**

While directly generating complex visualizations from text is still an area of active development, the trend is towards LLMs that can provide the data and descriptions needed for visualization tools, bridging the gap between textual data and visual representation.

Automating Administrative Tasks

Like it or not! Scrum Masters often must deal with various administrative tasks, which can be time-consuming. Prompt engineering can help to automate some of these tasks, freeing up the Scrum Master to focus on more strategic activities.

Meeting Scheduling and Note-Taking: Prompts can assist in scheduling meetings and generating meeting notes. This can save the Scrum Master significant time and effort.

Examples:

Prompt: "Schedule a Sprint Retrospective meeting with the development team and the product owner. The meeting should be 1 hour long and take place at the end of the sprint (Friday at 3:00 PM)."

Output: **`"Subject: Sprint Retrospective Meeting. Attendees: [Development Team], [Product Owner]. Date: [Date]. Time: 3:00 PM- 4:00 PM. Location: [Meeting Room/Virtual Meeting Link]"`**

Prompt: "Generate meeting notes from the following Sprint Planning discussion: [Sprint Planning Transcript]"

Output: **"Meeting Notes: Sprint Planning. Objectives: Define sprint goal and plan the work for the sprint. Decisions: Sprint Goal: [Sprint Goal]. User Stories: [List of User Stories]. Action Items: [List of Action Items]"**

There are AI-powered scheduling tools that can automatically find the best time for a meeting based on the availability of all participants. Similarly, AI note-taking tools can transcribe and summarize meetings in real-time. Scrum Masters can use these tools to automate meeting-related tasks.

Tracking Action Items: Prompts can help Scrum Masters track action items from various meetings and ensure that they are followed up on. This improves accountability and ensures that important tasks are not forgotten.

Examples:

Prompt: "Extract action items from the following meeting notes: [Meeting Notes]"

Output: **"Action Items: 1. John to create the database schema (Due: [Date]). 2. Sarah to design the user interface (Due: [Date]). 3. David to investigate the API integration issue (Due: [Date])"**

Prompt: "Generate a reminder email for John about the action item to create the database schema, which is due tomorrow."

Output: **"Subject: Reminder: Action Item Due Tomorrow. Hi John, This is a friendly reminder that the action item to create the database schema is due tomorrow. Please let me know if you have any questions or need any assistance. Thanks!"**

LLMs are being integrated into task management tools to automate the tracking and follow-up of action items. Scrum Masters can use these tools to streamline their task management workflows.

Managing Team Resources: Prompts can assist Scrum Masters in managing team resources, such as time and availability. This can help to optimize team capacity and ensure that work is distributed effectively.

Examples:

Prompt: "Analyze the team's availability for the next sprint, considering any planned time off or other commitments: [*Team Availability Data*]"

Output: **"Team Availability Analysis: John has 2 days of planned time off. Sarah is available full-time. David has a training course for 1 day. Overall, the team has [Number] of available days for the next sprint."**

Prompt: "Suggest an optimal distribution of user stories among the team members, considering their skills and availability: [*User Stories*], [*Team Member Skills*], [*Team Availability*]"

Output: **"Suggested User Story Distribution: John: User Story 1 (Database). Sarah: User Story 2 (UI Design). David: User Story 3 (API Integration). This distribution aligns with their respective skills and takes into account John's time off."**

As LLMs become more sophisticated, they could be used to predict potential resource conflicts and suggest proactive solutions, further optimizing team resource management.

Good to Remember:

i. **Embrace a Learning Mindset**: Prompt engineering is an evolving skill. Continuously experiment, learn from your results, and stay updated on the latest AI capabilities and prompting techniques.

ii. **Understand Your AI Tools**: Familiarize yourself with the specific AI tools your team is using and their strengths and limitations. Different models may respond best to different prompting styles.

iii. **Focus on Clarity and Specificity**: Just like in traditional Scrum, clear communication is key. Be precise in your prompts to guide the AI towards the desired outcome.

iv. **Leverage Examples:** When instructions alone are not enough, provide relevant examples to demonstrate the expected format, style, and content.

v. **Iterate and Refine**: Don't expect perfect results from the first prompt. Be prepared to iterate and refine your prompts based on the AI's output.

vi. **Collaborate and Share**: Share successful prompts and learnings with your team and the broader Scrum Master community.

vii. **Focus on Value**: Always consider how prompt engineering can help you deliver more value to your team and stakeholders, whether it's through improved facilitation, better insights, or streamlined processes.

Building on the foundation laid in this chapter, the next chapter shifts our focus to another critical role/accountability within Agile teams: the Product Owner. We'll delve into how Product Owners can harness the power of prompt engineering to refine their product vision, manage the product backlog with greater efficiency, and cultivate a deeper understanding of user needs.

Prepare to discover how AI can become an invaluable ally in the hands of a skilled Product Owner, shaping the future of product development in the Agile world.

Chapter 5

Prompt Engineering For Product Owners

This chapter delves into how Product Owners can effectively use prompt engineering to refine their product vision and strategy, manage the product backlog, gather and analyze user feedback, define features, and plan releases.

Product Owner, as we know it is the Value Maximizer for the Scrum Team.

Prompt engineering, the art and science of crafting effective instructions for AI models to elicit desired outputs, becomes a critical skill in this evolving landscape. Its application across the software development lifecycle can manifest in numerous ways, directly impacting Product Management and Product Ownership:

Enhanced User Research and Insights: Prompt engineering can be leveraged to analyze vast amounts of user data – including surveys, feedback forms, social media discussions, and support tickets– to identify emerging trends, pain points, and unmet needs with unprecedented speed and scale. Product

Managers can use carefully crafted prompts to extract nuanced insights, segment users based on specific criteria, and even predict future user behaviour, leading to more data-driven product decisions. For example, a prompt could be: "*Analyze these 10,000 customer reviews and identify the top three recurring pain points related to [specific feature] and suggest potential solutions.*"

Refined Product Vision and Strategy: By using prompts to explore different market scenarios, competitive strategies, and technological possibilities, Product Managers can gain a more comprehensive understanding of the strategic landscape. They can use LLMs to generate potential product visions based on identified trends or to evaluate the feasibility and potential impact of different strategic directions. Prompts like: "Based on current market trends in [industry] and the capabilities of [emerging technology], generate three potential product visions for the next five years" can be invaluable.

Automated Requirements Elicitation and Documentation: Product Owners spend significant time gathering, documenting, and refining user stories and requirements. Prompt engineering can streamline this process. By providing LLMs with context about user needs and product goals, Product Owners can generate initial drafts of user stories, acceptance criteria, and even technical specifications. For instance, a prompt could be: "Based on the user need 'As a user, I want to be able to track my order status so that I know when it will arrive,' generate three detailed user stories with specific acceptance criteria." This automation frees up Product Owners to focus on more complex aspects of stakeholder management and team collaboration.

Intelligent Prioritization: Prioritizing features is a core responsibility of Product Owners. Prompt engineering can assist in this by analyzing various factors like business value, development effort, risk, and dependencies. By feeding this data into an LLM with well-defined prompts, Product Owners can receive data-driven recommendations for feature prioritization, facilitating more objective and efficient decision-making. A prompt example: "Given the following features with their estimated business value, development effort, and dependencies, suggest a prioritized backlog for the next sprint, justifying the order."

Streamlined Backlog Management: Maintaining a well-groomed product backlog is crucial for Agile development. Prompt engineering can help Product Owners in tasks such as breaking down epics into smaller user stories, identifying potential dependencies, and ensuring that backlog items are clearly articulated and ready for development. Prompts like: "Break down the epic 'Implement user authentication' into smaller, independent user stories with clear acceptance criteria" can significantly improve backlog efficiency.

Enhanced Collaboration with Development Teams: The excerpt explicitly mentions "seamless collaboration between development teams and LLMs." Product Owners can act as orchestrators in this collaboration, using prompt engineering to facilitate communication and understanding between the development team and the AI. For example, a Product Owner could use prompts to generate code examples or explanations based on user stories, helping developers better understand the intended functionality. Similarly, developers can use prompts to clarify requirements or identify potential implementation challenges, which the Product Owner can then address.

Automated Testing and Quality Assurance: The vision of "bugs becoming relics of the past" is ambitious but highlights the potential of AI in quality assurance. Product Owners can collaborate with QA teams to use prompt engineering to generate test cases based on user stories and acceptance criteria. LLMs can also analyze code and identify potential vulnerabilities or areas of concern, contributing to a more robust and reliable product.

A prompt example for test case generation: "Generate five positive and three negative test cases for the user story 'As a user, I can reset my password using my email address.'"

Data-Driven Product Iteration: Prompt engineering can facilitate the analysis of post-release product usage data. Product Managers and Owners can use prompts to identify areas of the product that are performing well, areas that need improvement, and opportunities for new features based on user behaviour. This data-driven approach, augmented by AI insights, enables faster and more effective product iteration.

So, let's explore how can Prompt Engineering help the Product Owners to go to the next level of value delivery. Here are some core areas where Product Owners can effectively use prompt engineering:

Enhancing User Understanding and Empathy:

Generating Diverse User Personas: Instead of relying solely on static personas, prompt engineering can help create a wider range of nuanced personas based on different behavioural patterns, motivations, and pain points.

How?: By providing a basic persona template (e.g., "A [age] [profession] named [name] who [goal] but struggles with [problem]"), you can prompt the LLM to generate variations with different demographics, motivations, and frustrations.

Example Prompt: "Generate three distinct user personas for a mobile application designed for learning a new language. Each persona should include their age, profession, primary motivation for learning a language, key challenges they face, and their technical proficiency level."

Value: This allows Product Owners to consider a broader spectrum of user needs and design more inclusive and effective solutions.

Analyzing large volumes of user feedback (surveys, reviews, support tickets) can be time-consuming. Prompt engineering can help extract key themes, sentiment, and pain points efficiently.

How?: By providing the feedback data and specific instructions, you can prompt the LLM to identify recurring issues, positive aspects, and feature requests.

Example Prompt: "Analyze the following customer reviews for our project management software and identify the top three most frequently mentioned pain points and the overall sentiment (positive, negative, neutral) associated with each."

Value: This enables Product Owners to quickly understand user needs and prioritize product improvements based on data-driven insights.

Simulating User Interviews and Scenarios: Prompting LLMs to simulate user interviews based on specific scenarios can provide valuable insights into user behaviour and preferences without the need for extensive real-world interviews.

How?: By defining a user persona, a specific task or problem, and the desired interaction style, you can prompt the LLM to role-play the user and provide their perspective.

Example Prompt: "Simulate a user interview with a project manager who is trying to onboard their team to our new collaboration platform. Ask questions about their current workflow, their expectations from the new platform, and any potential challenges they foresee."

Value: This can help Product Owners anticipate user questions, identify potential usability issues, and refine user onboarding processes.

LLMs can assist in brainstorming and structuring empathy maps and user journey maps based on user research data or generated personas.

How?: By providing information about a user persona and their interaction with the product, you can prompt the LLM to suggest elements for each stage of the map (e.g., what the user thinks, feels, says, and does).

Example Prompt: "Based on the persona of 'Sarah, a busy marketing manager trying to schedule social media posts,' create an outline for a user journey map for the task of scheduling a week's worth of posts using our platform. Include key stages, user actions, potential pain points, and opportunities for improvement."

Value: This helps Product Owners visualize the user experience and identify areas for optimization.

Defining and Refining Product Vision and Strategy:

Brainstorming Product Ideas and Features: Overcoming creative blocks is a common challenge. Prompt engineering can facilitate brainstorming sessions by generating a wide range of product ideas and features based on specific goals or user needs.

How?: By providing a core problem statement or a desired outcome, you can prompt the LLM to suggest potential solutions or features.

Example Prompt: "Our goal is to increase user engagement with our fitness tracking app. Generate ten different feature ideas that could motivate users to track their activity more consistently."

Value: This can spark new ideas and help Product Owners explore different product directions.

Analyzing Market Trends and Competitor Analysis: Prompting LLMs to summarize market research reports or analyze competitor offerings can provide valuable insights for strategic decision-making.

How?: By providing links to reports or competitor websites, you can prompt the LLM to extract key trends, identify competitive advantages, and highlight potential opportunities.

Example Prompt: "Summarize the key trends and predictions from this market research report on the future of e-commerce [link to report]. Also, analyze the pricing strategies of our top three competitors in the online grocery delivery space [links to competitor websites]."

Value: This helps Product Owners stay informed about the market landscape and identify potential competitive advantages.

Crafting and Refining Product Vision Statements: A clear and compelling product vision is crucial. Prompt engineering can assist in drafting and refining vision statements by exploring different angles and ensuring clarity and impact.

How?: By providing the core purpose and target audience of the product, you can prompt the LLM to generate several variations of a vision statement.

Example Prompt: "Our product aims to help small businesses manage their finances more effectively. Generate three different versions of a concise and inspiring product vision statement."

Value: This helps Product Owners articulate the product's purpose and direction effectively.

Defining and Prioritizing Product Backlog Items: Prompt engineering can assist in breaking down large features into smaller, manageable user stories and defining clear acceptance criteria. It can also help in prioritizing backlog items based on various factors.

How?: By providing a high-level feature description, you can prompt the LLM to suggest potential user stories and acceptance criteria. You can also provide prioritization frameworks (e.g., RICE, MoSCoW) and ask the LLM to apply them based on given criteria.

Example Prompt: "Break down the feature 'User profile management' into several smaller user stories with clear acceptance criteria. Consider different aspects like updating personal information, changing passwords, and managing notification preferences."

Value: This helps Product Owners create a well-defined and prioritized product backlog.

Enhancing Communication and Collaboration:

Generating Clear and Concise Product Documentation: Writing product specifications, user guides, and release notes can be time-consuming. Prompt engineering can help generate initial drafts or refine existing documentation for clarity and conciseness.

How?: By providing the key information and desired tone, you can prompt the LLM to generate different types of product documentation.

Example Prompt: "Write a concise set of release notes for the latest version of our mobile app, highlighting the new features, bug fixes, and known issues. Use a friendly and informative tone."

Value: This saves time and ensures consistent and clear communication with stakeholders and users.

Crafting Effective Communication for Stakeholders: Product Owners need to communicate effectively with various stakeholders (engineering, design, marketing, executives). Prompt engineering can help tailor communication for different audiences.

How?: By specifying the audience and the key message, you can prompt the LLM to generate emails, presentations, or status updates in an appropriate tone and format.

Example Prompt: "Write a brief email update for the executive team on the progress of the 'new user onboarding flow' project. Highlight key milestones achieved and any potential roadblocks."

Value: This ensures clear and impactful communication with all stakeholders.

Facilitating Brainstorming and Ideation Sessions: Prompt engineering can be used during team meetings to stimulate creative thinking and generate new ideas.

How?: By posing open-ended questions or providing specific challenges, you can prompt the LLM to offer diverse perspectives and potential solutions.

Example Prompt: "We are looking for innovative ways to improve collaboration within our remote teams. Generate five unconventional ideas we could explore."

Value: This can enhance team collaboration and lead to more creative solutions.

Summarizing Meeting Notes and Action Items: After meetings, prompt engineering can help quickly summarize key discussion points and identify action items.

How?: By providing the meeting transcript or notes, you can prompt the LLM to extract the main topics discussed, key decisions made, and assigned action items.

Example Prompt: "Summarize the key discussion points and list all the action items with assigned owners and deadlines from the following meeting transcript [paste transcript here]."

Value: This improves meeting efficiency and ensures clear follow-up on action items.

Streamlining Product Development Processes:

Generating User Story Examples and Templates: Prompt engineering can help create consistent and well-structured user stories by providing examples and templates based on best practices.

How?: By specifying the type of user story (e.g., feature, bug fix) and the desired format, you can prompt the LLM to generate examples.

Example Prompt: "Provide three examples of well-written user stories for a new e-commerce platform feature that allows users to save items to a wishlist. Each story should follow the 'As a [user type], I want [goal] so that [benefit]' format and include clear acceptance criteria."

Value: This ensures consistency and clarity in user story writing.

Assisting with Test Case Generation: Prompt engineering can help generate potential test cases based on user stories and acceptance criteria, saving time and ensuring broader test coverage.

How?: By providing a user story and its acceptance criteria, you can prompt the LLM to suggest relevant test scenarios and edge cases.

Example Prompt: "Generate a list of potential test cases for the following user story: 'As a registered user, I want to be able to reset my password so that I can regain access to my account if I forget1 it.' Consider both positive and negative scenarios."

Value: This improves the efficiency and effectiveness of the testing process.

Analyzing and Summarizing Technical Documentation: Product Owners often need to understand technical aspects of the product. Prompt engineering can help summarize and explain complex technical documentation.

How?: By providing the technical documentation, you can prompt the LLM to explain specific concepts or summarize key information in a more accessible way.

Example Prompt: "Explain the core functionality of the 'API integration layer' described in the following technical document in simple terms that a non-technical stakeholder can understand [link to document]."

Value: This facilitates better communication and understanding between technical and non-technical teams.

Identifying Potential Risks and Dependencies: When planning product development, prompt engineering can assist in identifying potential risks and dependencies associated with specific features or initiatives.

How?: By providing a description of a feature or project, you can prompt the LLM to brainstorm potential risks and dependencies that need to be considered.

Example Prompt: "We are planning to integrate a third-party payment gateway into our application. What are some potential risks and dependencies we should consider during the planning phase?"

Value: This helps Product Owners proactively address potential challenges and ensure smoother development.

Continuous Learning and Improvement:

Staying Updated on Industry Trends: Prompt engineering can help Product Owners stay informed about the latest industry trends, best practices, and emerging technologies by summarizing relevant articles and reports.

How?: By providing links to articles or specifying areas of interest, you can prompt the LLM to provide summaries and key takeaways.

Example Prompt: "Summarize the key insights from these three articles on the latest trends in SaaS product management [links to articles]."

Value: This helps Product Owners stay competitive and identify potential opportunities for innovation.

Analyzing Product Performance Data: Prompt engineering can assist in analyzing product analytics data to identify areas for improvement and understand user behaviour patterns.

How?: By providing key metrics and data points, you can prompt the LLM to identify trends, anomalies, and potential areas for investigation.

Example Prompt: "Analyze the following user engagement data for our key features over the past month and identify any significant trends or areas where user engagement is low."

Value: This enables data-driven decision-making and continuous product improvement.

Generating Ideas for A/B Tests and Experiments: Prompt engineering can help brainstorm hypotheses and design A/B tests to validate product assumptions and optimize user experience.

How?: By identifying a specific problem or area for improvement, you can prompt the LLM to suggest potential A/B test variations and hypotheses.

Example Prompt: "We want to increase the click-through rate on our primary call-to-action button. Generate three different variations of the button text and a hypothesis for each."

Value: This facilitates a data-driven approach to product optimization.

Reflecting on Past Product Decisions and Outcomes: Prompting LLMs to analyze past product decisions and their outcomes can provide valuable lessons learned and inform future strategies.

How?: By providing context about a past decision and its results, you can prompt the LLM to identify contributing factors, potential alternative approaches, and key takeaways.

Example Prompt: "We decided to prioritize feature X over feature Y six months ago, and user adoption of feature X has been lower than expected. Analyze the potential reasons for this outcome and suggest lessons learned for future prioritization decisions."

Value: This fosters a culture of continuous learning and improvement within the product team.

Great!

Now you have a good understanding of how Product Owners may leverage Prompt Engineering in their day to day activities, let us deep-dive into scenarios where Prompt Engineering saves the day!

Product Vision and Strategy

Product Owners are responsible for defining the product vision and strategy, which serves as a guiding light for the development team. Prompt engineering can be a valuable tool in this process.

Generating Product Vision Statements

Product vision statements articulate the long-term goal of the product. Prompts can help Product Owners explore different facets of the vision and generate compelling statements.

Examples:

Prompt: "Write a product vision statement for a mobile application that helps users track their personal finances."

Output: **"Empower individuals to achieve financial well-being through an intuitive and comprehensive mobile application that simplifies budgeting, spending tracking, and financial planning."**

"To be the leading mobile platform that provides personalized financial insights and tools, enabling users to make informed decisions and secure their financial future."

Prompt: "Generate a short and impactful product vision statement for an online learning platform."

Output: **"To democratize education by providing accessible and engaging online learning experiences for everyone, everywhere."**

A Product Owner can brainstorm various product vision statements. The LLM's suggestions can help the team to identify a vision that is both inspiring and aligned with their business goals.

Analyzing Market Trends and Competitor Data: Product Owners need to stay informed about market trends and competitor activities. Prompts can assist in analyzing data and extracting key insights.

Examples:

Prompt: "Analyze the following market research data on the fitness tracker industry and identify the top 3 emerging trends: [*Market Research Data*]"

Output: **"Top 3 emerging trends: 1. Increased focus on personalized fitness plans. 2. Integration with mental wellness features. 3. Growing demand for affordable fitness trackers."**

Prompt: "Compare and contrast the following competitor products ([*Competitor A*], [*Competitor B*], [*Competitor C*]) and identify their strengths and weaknesses."

Output: **"Competitor A: Strength - Strong brand recognition. Weakness - Limited feature set. Competitor B: Strength - Innovative features. Weakness - High price point. Competitor C: Strength - User-friendly interface. Weakness - Poor customer support."**

Market research firms are increasingly using AI tools to analyze large datasets and generate reports. Product Owners can leverage these tools, powered by prompt engineering, to gain a deeper understanding of the market landscape.

Creating Product Roadmaps: Product roadmaps visualize the evolution of the product over time. Prompts can help Product Owners generate roadmap themes, epics, and features.

Examples:

Prompt: "Generate a product roadmap for the next 6 months for an e-commerce platform, focusing on improving the user experience."

Output:

"Q1: Theme: Enhance Navigation

Epic 1: Redesign Homepage

Feature 1: Improved search functionality

Feature 2: Personalized product recommendations

Theme: Streamline Checkout Process

Epic 2: Simplify Payment Options

Feature 3: One-click checkout

Feature 4: Guest checkout"

Prompt: "Define the key milestones for a product roadmap focused on launching a new social media platform."

Output: **"Key milestones: 1. MVP launch with core features (user profiles, posting, feed). 2. Implementation of direct messaging. 3. Introduction of group features. 4. Monetization strategy implementation."**

User Story Management

Product Owners are responsible for defining and managing user stories, which are the building blocks of the product backlog. Prompt engineering can significantly enhance user story management.

Writing User Stories from Various Perspectives: User stories describe a feature from the perspective of the end-user. Prompts can help Product Owners write user stories that capture the needs and goals of different user roles.

Examples:

Prompt: "Write a user story for a library management system from the perspective of a librarian."

Output: **"As a librarian, I want to be able to easily catalogue new books into the system, so that I can efficiently manage the library's collection."**

Prompt: "Write a user story for an online food delivery app from the perspective of a customer with dietary restrictions."

Output: **"As a customer with dietary restrictions, I want to be able to filter restaurants and menu items based on my dietary needs (e.g., gluten-free, vegan), so that I can easily find suitable food options."**

Defining Acceptance Criteria and Test Cases:

Acceptance criteria define the conditions that must be met for a user story to be considered complete. Prompts can assist in generating clear and testable acceptance criteria, as well as corresponding test cases.

Examples:

Prompt: "Write acceptance criteria for the user story 'As a customer, I want to be able to reset my password, so that I can regain access to my account if I forget it.'"

Output: **"Verify that the user can initiate the password reset process by providing their email address."**

"Verify that the system sends a password reset link to the user's email address."

"Verify that the user can create a new password using the reset link."

"Verify that the user is able to log in with their new password."

Prompt: "Generate test cases for the acceptance criteria above."

Output:

"Test Case 1: Verify that the password reset link is valid and functional."

"Test Case 2: Verify that the system enforces password complexity requirements."

"Test Case 3: Verify that the user receives an error message if they enter an invalid email address."

Prioritizing and Refining the Product Backlog: Product Owners are responsible for prioritizing the product backlog, ensuring that the most valuable features are delivered first. Prompts can help in analyzing user feedback, business value, and technical feasibility to inform prioritization decisions. Prompts can also assist in refining backlog items to ensure they are clear, concise, and actionable.

Examples:

Prompt: "Prioritize the following user stories ([*User Story A*], [*User Story B*], [*User Story C*]) based on their business value and user impact."

Output: **"Prioritized User Stories: 1. User Story B (High business value, high user impact). 2. User Story A (Medium business value, medium user impact). 3. User Story C (Low business value, low user impact)."**

Prompt: "Refine the following user story: 'Add a button to the page.' Provide more detail and clarity."

Output: **"As a user, I want a clearly labelled 'Add to Cart' button on the product details page, positioned below the product description and above the customer reviews, so that I can easily add the product to my shopping cart."**

Gathering and Analyzing User Feedback

Understanding user needs and pain points is crucial for building successful products. Prompt engineering can facilitate the process of gathering and analyzing user feedback.

Summarizing User Interviews and Surveys: Product Owners often conduct user interviews and surveys to gather feedback. Prompts can help to summarize the key findings from these interactions, saving time and effort.

Examples:

Prompt: "Summarize the following transcript of a user interview: [*User Interview Transcript*]"

Output: "Key findings from the user interview: The user found the interface to be intuitive but expressed frustration with the slow loading times. They also suggested adding a dark mode option."

Prompt: "Analyze the following survey results and identify the top 3 user pain points: [*Survey Results*]"

Output: **"Top 3 user pain points: 1. Difficulty finding specific products. 2. Confusing navigation. 3. Lack of mobile responsiveness."**

Identifying User Needs and Pain Points: Prompts can help Product Owners to delve deeper into user feedback and identify the underlying needs and pain points. This understanding is essential for developing solutions that truly address user problems.

Examples:

Prompt: "Based on the following user feedback ('The search function is terrible! I can never find what I'm looking for'), identify the user's underlying need and pain point."

Output: **"Underlying need: The user needs to be able to quickly and easily find products. Pain point: Frustration with the ineffective search function, leading to wasted time and a poor user experience."**

Prompt: "Analyze the following user feedback and identify common needs and pain points related to the mobile app's onboarding process: [*User Feedback on Onboarding*]"

Output: **"Common needs: Clear instructions, a quick and easy setup, and a sense of value from the app. Pain points: Confusing steps, excessive information requests, and lack of clarity on the app's core benefits."**

Generating User Personas and Journey Maps: User personas are fictional representations of ideal users, while user journey maps visualize the user's interaction with the product. Prompts can assist in creating these valuable tools for user-centric design.

Examples:

Prompt: "Generate a user persona for a user of a language learning app, based on the following characteristics: [*User Characteristics*]"

Output: **"User Persona: Name: Maria Rodriguez. Age: 25. Occupation: Student. Goals: To become fluent in Spanish for travel and career opportunities. Pain Points: Lack of time for traditional language classes, difficulty finding engaging learning materials."**

Prompt: "Create a user journey map for a user purchasing a product on an e-commerce website."

Output: **"(The LLM can outline the steps of the journey) User Journey Map: 1. User visits the website. 2. User searches for a product. 3. User views product details. 4. User adds product to cart. 5. User proceeds**

to checkout. 6. User completes the purchase. 7. User receives order confirmation."

Feature Definition and Experimentation

Product Owners are responsible for defining new features and experimenting to validate their value. Prompt engineering can be a valuable aid in this process.

Brainstorming New Feature Ideas: Prompts can help Product Owners generate a wide range of feature ideas, encouraging creativity and exploration.

Examples:

Prompt: "Brainstorm new feature ideas for a music streaming app, focusing on enhancing the social experience."

Output: **"Feature Ideas: 1. Collaborative playlists. 2. In-app messaging with friends. 3. Sharing listening activity on social media. 4. Live listening parties."**

Prompt: "Generate innovative feature concepts for a smart home device.

Output: **"Feature Concepts: 1. Predictive energy consumption management. 2. Automated personalized lighting scenarios. 3. Integrated pet monitoring and interaction."**

Creating Feature Specifications: Feature specifications describe the details of a feature, including its functionality, user interface, and behaviour. Prompts can assist in generating comprehensive and well-structured specifications.

Examples:

Prompt: "Write a feature specification for a 'dark mode' feature in a mobile app."

Output: **"(The LLM can outline the different sections of the specification) Feature Specification: 1. Feature Description. 2. User Interface. 3. Functionality. 4. Error Handling. 5. Performance Requirements."**

Prompt: "Generate a detailed feature specification for a shopping cart functionality on an e-commerce website."

Output: **"(The LLM can provide details on aspects like) Feature Specification: Includes sections on product addition, quantity updates, total price calculation, discount application, and error handling for invalid inputs or stock issues."**

Designing A/B Tests: A/B tests are used to compare different versions of a feature and determine which one performs best. Prompts can help Product Owners design effective A/B tests, including defining the variations, metrics, and target audience.

Examples:

Prompt: "Design an A/B test to compare two different call-to-action buttons on a landing page."

Output: **"A/B Test Design: Variation A: 'Get Started' button. Variation B: 'Sign Up Free' button. Metric: Click-through rate. Target Audience: New website visitors."**

Prompt: "Generate an A/B test plan to evaluate the impact of two different pricing strategies on user conversion rates for a subscription service."

Output: **"A/B Test Plan: Details on the control group, experimental group(s) with different pricing models, key metrics like conversion rate and customer lifetime value, and the planned duration of the experiment."**

Release Planning and Documentation

Product Owners are involved in planning product releases and creating documentation. Prompt engineering can help to streamline these tasks.

Generating Release Notes: Release notes communicate the changes and improvements included in a new product release. Prompts can assist in generating clear and concise release notes for different audiences.

Examples:

Prompt: "Generate release notes for a new version of a mobile app, targeting end-users."

Output: **"Release Notes: What's New: - Added dark mode. - Improved search functionality. - Fixed a bug that caused the app to crash on some devices."**

Prompt: "Create detailed release notes for internal stakeholders, focusing on technical changes and bug fixes."

Output: **"Release Notes: Includes sections on API updates, database schema changes, specific bug fixes with issue tracking IDs, and known limitations."**

Creating User Documentation and Tutorials: User documentation and tutorials help users to understand how to use the product. Prompts can assist in creating clear, concise, and helpful documentation.

Examples:

Prompt: "Write a user tutorial on how to use the new 'dark mode' feature in a mobile app."

Output: **"(The LLM can provide step-by-step instructions) User Tutorial: 1. Open the app settings. 2. Tap on 'Display'. 3. Select 'Dark Mode'."**

Prompt: "Generate a FAQ document for a software application, addressing common user questions."

Output: **"FAQ: Includes questions and answers on installation, basic usage, troubleshooting common errors, and contact information for support."**

The future of product development is not just about what we build, but how we build it. As we move to the next chapter, we'll explore how prompt engineering can be applied to the entire software development lifecycle, moving beyond specific roles to revolutionize the development process itself.

Good to Remember:

i. **Maintain the Human Touch and Context**: While AI can automate and augment tasks, it cannot replace the critical human elements of understanding user empathy, navigating complex stakeholder relationships, and making nuanced strategic decisions. Avoid blindly accepting AI-generated outputs without critical evaluation and validation.

ii. **Focus on Clarity and Precision in Prompt Crafting**: Applies to every role, while using prompts. The quality of the output from an LLM is directly proportional to the quality of the prompt. Ambiguous or poorly defined prompts will likely lead to irrelevant or inaccurate outputs, wasting time and effort. Experiment with different phrasing and parameters to optimize prompt effectiveness.

iii. **Iterate and Refine Prompts Based on Feedback:** Prompt engineering is an iterative process. The initial prompts may not always yield the desired results. Product Owners should be prepared to analyze the AI's output, identify areas for improvement in the prompt, and refine it accordingly. Furthermore, collaborate with Developers and other Stakeholders to gather feedback on the usefulness and accuracy of AI-generated content.

iv. **Understand the Limitations and Biases of LLMs:** It's essential to recognize that LLMs are trained on vast amounts of data, which may contain biases. Product Owners should be aware of these potential biases and critically evaluate AI-generated insights, especially when dealing with user research or strategic analysis. Avoid relying solely on AI outputs without considering potential biases and ensuring fairness and inclusivity. Additionally, understand the inherent limitations of current LLM technology; they are powerful tools but not substitutes for human creativity and critical thinking.

v. **Integrate Prompt Engineering into Existing Workflows Gradually:** The adoption of prompt engineering should be a gradual process, integrated thoughtfully into existing product development workflows. Start with specific use cases where AI can provide immediate value and then progressively expand its application as the team gains experience and confidence. Provide adequate training and support to Product Owners and the development team to ensure effective utilization of these new tools and techniques.

Avoid a sudden, disruptive выполнение (implementation) that could overwhelm the team and hinder productivity.

Now, that you are armed with techniques to leverage prompt engineering for Scrum Master and Product Owner, get ready to witness how AI-driven prompts can orchestrate seamless collaboration between Developers and LLMs, promising an era where code writes itself and bugs become relics of the past.

Chapter 6

Prompt Engineering For Developers

Imagine a world where coding is less about wrestling with syntax and more about expressing your creative vision. What if you could describe complex software functionality in plain English and watch the AI bring it to life?

This isn't science fiction; it's the growing reality of prompt engineering for developers. This chapter will take you on a journey into the heart of how Large Language Models (LLMs), guided by skilfully crafted prompts, are revolutionizing the way software is built. Prepare to have your perceptions of coding challenged as we explore how AI can become your most powerful coding partner, boosting your productivity, unleashing your creativity, and fundamentally reshaping the developer experience. From generating elegant code snippets to demystifying cryptic legacy systems, the future of development is being written with prompts.

And Hello, this ain't your grandpa's coding manual. We're diving headfirst into the wild, wonderful world of prompt engineering for developers – and trust me, it's about to get lit!

Forget endless boilerplate and soul-crushing debugging; the future's here, and it's powered by the magic words we whisper to our AI overlords (who are actually pretty chill).

So, let's get started with how Prompt Engineering is being leveraged by Developers world-wide in day-to-day activities:

Empowering Coders:

Code Generation and Completion:

Generating Code Snippets: Prompting for specific functionalities in various programming languages.

How? Providing clear instructions on the desired functionality, input/output specifications, and sometimes even the programming paradigm.

Example Prompt (Python):

Write a Python function that takes a list of integers as input and returns the sum of all even numbers in the list.

Value: Speeds up development by providing starting points or handling repetitive coding tasks.

Full Function/Class Generation: Describing the overall purpose and structure of a code module.

How? Providing a high-level description of the component's responsibilities, dependencies, and expected behaviour.

Example Prompt (Java):

Generate a Java class representing a 'ShoppingCart' with methods to add items, remove items, calculate the total price, and apply discounts.

Value: Can accelerate the creation of boilerplate code and complex structures.

Code Completion and Suggestion: Leveraging LLMs integrated into IDEs for intelligent suggestions.

How? The LLM analyzes the context of the code being written and suggests relevant completions, variable names, or even entire code blocks.

Example Scenario: A developer starts typing a function to handle file I/O, and the LLM suggests the necessary import statements and common file handling patterns.

Value: Improves coding speed and reduces the likelihood of syntax errors.

Cross-Language Translation: Converting code from one programming language to another.

How? Providing the source code and specifying the target language.

Example Prompt:

Translate the following JavaScript code to Python:

`function greet(name) { console.log('Hello, ' + name); }`

Value: Facilitates working with polyglot systems or migrating codebases.

Understanding and Explaining Existing Code: Prompting for explanations of unfamiliar code blocks.

How? Providing the code snippet and asking for a breakdown of it's functionality, logic, and purpose.

Example Prompt:

Explain what this regular expression does:

`^([a-zA-Z0-9._%+-]+)@([a-zA-Z0-9.-]+)\.([a-zA-Z]{2,})$`

Value: Helps developers quickly understand legacy code or code written by others.

Code Refactoring and Optimization:

Suggesting Code Improvements: Prompting for ways to make code more readable, efficient, or maintainable.

How? Providing the code and asking for refactoring suggestions based on best practices.

Example Prompt (Python):

Refactor this Python code to improve it's readability and efficiency: `results = []; for i in range(len(data)): if data[i] > 5: results.append(data[i] * 2)`

Value: Leads to higher-quality and more maintainable codebases.

Identifying Potential Bugs and Vulnerabilities: Prompting for security or logical flaws in the code.

How? Providing the code and asking for potential issues.

Example Prompt (JavaScript):

Analyze this JavaScript code for potential security vulnerabilities: `app.post('/login', (req, res) => { const username = req.body.username; const password = req.body.password; // ... database query using username and password ... });`

Value: Helps catch errors and security risks early in the development cycle.

Generating Unit Tests: Prompting for test cases to ensure code functionality.

How? Providing the code and asking for relevant unit tests covering different scenarios.

Example Prompt (JUnit):

Generate JUnit test cases for the following Java function that calculates the factorial of a non-negative integer.

Value: Improves code reliability and reduces the risk of regressions.

Learning and Problem Solving:

Understanding Complex Concepts: Prompting for explanations of technical topics and frameworks.

How? Asking specific questions about concepts or providing documentation and asking for clarification.

Example Prompt:

Explain the concept of 'dependency injection' in the context of Spring Framework.

Value: Accelerates learning and helps developers grasp new technologies.

Debugging Assistance: Describing errors and asking for potential causes and solutions.

How? Providing error messages, relevant code snippets, and a description of the problem.

Example Prompt:

I'm getting a 'TypeError: Cannot read property 'undefined' of null' error in this JavaScript code: `const user = data.profile.name; console.log(user);` What could be the possible causes?

Value: Helps developers troubleshoot issues more efficiently.

Finding Relevant Documentation and Resources: Prompting for links to specific information.

How? Asking targeted questions about where to find information on a particular topic or technology.

Example Prompt:

Where can I find the official documentation for the React Router library?

Value: Saves time searching for necessary resources.

Supercharging Testers:

Test Case Generation:

Generating Functional Test Cases: Prompting for test scenarios based on user stories or requirements.

How? Providing a user story or a functional specification and asking for relevant test cases.

Example Prompt:

Generate functional test cases for the user story: 'As a user, I want to be able to filter products by price range on the product listing page.'

Value: Ensures comprehensive test coverage based on requirements.

Generating Edge Case and Boundary Value Tests: Prompting for tests that explore unusual or extreme inputs.

How? Providing the functionality and asking for test cases that push the boundaries of expected input.

Example Prompt:

Generate edge case test inputs for a function that calculates the square root of a number, considering negative numbers, zero, and very large numbers.

Value: Helps identify potential issues in less common scenarios.

Generating Performance and Load Test Scenarios: Prompting for simulations of high user load.

How? Describing the application and asking for scenarios to test it's performance under stress.

Example Prompt:

Generate load test scenarios for an e-commerce website during a flash sale, considering a large number of concurrent users accessing product pages and the checkout process.

Value: Helps ensure the application can handle expected and unexpected traffic.

Generating UI/UX Test Scenarios: Prompting for tests that focus on the user interface and experience.

How? Describing a UI element or user flow and asking for relevant test cases.

Example Prompt:

Generate UI test scenarios for the login form, considering different input combinations, error messages, and accessibility.

Value: Ensures a user-friendly and accessible application.

Test Data Generation:

Generating Realistic Test Data: Prompting for data that mimics real-world usage patterns.

How? Describing the data requirements and asking for the generation of diverse and realistic data sets.

Example Prompt:

Generate a set of 100 realistic user profiles with varying names, email addresses, locations, and purchase histories for testing an e-commerce platform.

Value: Improves the realism and effectiveness of testing.

Generating Specific Test Data for Edge Cases: Prompting for data tailored to specific test scenarios.

How? Describing the edge case and asking for data that triggers it.

Example Prompt:

Generate test data for a date input field that includes invalid date formats, dates outside the allowed range, and empty values.

Value: Facilitates targeted testing of specific conditions.

Test Script Generation and Automation:

Generating Basic Test Scripts: Prompting for initial versions of automated test scripts.

How? Providing the test case steps and the target automation framework.

Example Prompt (Selenium)**:**

Generate a basic Selenium script in Python to automate the test case: 'Verify that a user can successfully log in with valid credentials.'

Value: Provides a starting point for test automation efforts.

Suggesting Improvements to Existing Test Scripts: Prompting for ways to make test scripts more robust and efficient.

How? Providing the test script and asking for refactoring suggestions.

Example Prompt (Cypress)**:**

Refactor this Cypress test script to improve it's readability and reduce duplication.

Value: Leads to more maintainable and reliable automated tests.

Test Result Analysis and Reporting:

Summarizing Test Results: Prompting for concise summaries of test execution outcomes.

How? Providing test reports and asking for a summary of the key findings.

Example Prompt:

Summarize the results of the latest regression test suite, highlighting the number of tests passed, failed, and skipped, and identifying the key failure points.

Value: Helps quickly understand the overall quality of the software.

Identifying Root Causes of Test Failures: Prompting for potential reasons behind failed tests.

How? Providing error messages, logs, and relevant code snippets and asking for possible causes.

Example Prompt:

The following test case failed with a 'NullPointerException' in the 'UserService' class. Based on the stack trace, what could be the potential root causes?

Value: Accelerates the debugging process for failed tests.

Optimizing DevOps Practices:

Infrastructure as Code (IaC) Generation:

Generating Configuration Files: Prompting for basic infrastructure configurations in tools like Terraform or CloudFormation.

How? Describing the desired infrastructure components and their basic properties.

Example Prompt (Terraform**):**

Generate a basic Terraform configuration to create an AWS EC2 instance with a specified instance type and AMI.

Value: Simplifies the initial setup of infrastructure.

Modifying Existing IaC: Prompting for changes to existing infrastructure configurations.

How? Providing the current configuration and describing the desired modifications.

Example Prompt (CloudFormation):

Modify this CloudFormation template to add a new security group rule allowing inbound traffic on port 8080.

Value: Makes infrastructure updates easier and less error-prone.

Scripting and Automation:

Generating Shell Scripts: Prompting for scripts to automate common DevOps tasks.

How? Describing the task to be automated.

Example Prompt (Bash):

Write a Bash script that backs up all files in a specific directory to a remote server using SCP.

Value: Automates repetitive tasks, improving efficiency.

Generating Python or other Automation Scripts: Prompting for more complex automation logic.

How? Describing the desired automation workflow.

Example Prompt (Python):

Write a Python script that monitors the CPU utilization of a server and sends an alert if it exceeds a certain threshold for a specified period.

Value: Enables more sophisticated automation and monitoring.

Log Analysis and Monitoring:

Summarizing Log Files: Prompting for key information and patterns in log data.

How?: Providing log data and asking for a summary of important events.

Example Prompt:

Summarize the error messages and warnings in this server log file from the last 24 hours.

Value: Helps quickly identify issues and trends in system behaviour.

Generating Alerting Rules: Prompting for rules to trigger notifications based on log patterns or metrics.

How? Describing the conditions that should trigger an alert.

Example Prompt:

Generate an alerting rule for Prometheus that triggers when the CPU utilization of any server exceeds 90% for more than 5 minutes.

Value: Enables proactive monitoring and faster incident response.

Deployment and Release Management:

Generating Deployment Scripts: Prompting for scripts to automate application deployments.

How? Describing the deployment process and target environment.

Example Prompt (Ansible)**:**

Generate an Ansible playbook to deploy a Docker container to a remote Linux server.

Value: Automates the deployment process, reducing errors and downtime.

Generating Release Notes: Prompting for summaries of changes included in a release.

How? Providing a list of commit's or Jira tickets.

Example Prompt:

Generate release notes for the following list of Jira tickets, summarizing the key features and bug fixes included in this release [list of tickets].

Value: Streamlines the communication of release information.

Security and Compliance:

Generating Security Policies: Prompting for basic security guidelines.

How?: Describing the system or application.

Example Prompt:

Generate a basic password policy for a web application.

Value: Provides a starting point for security considerations.

Analyzing Security Scan Results: Prompting for summaries and explanations of security vulnerabilities.

How?: Providing security scan reports.

Example Prompt:

Summarize the high-severity vulnerabilities identified in this security scan report and suggest potential remediation steps.

Value: Helps prioritize and address security risks.

Well, now that you have a fair idea about how you can leverage prompt engineering as a Developer in a Scrum Team, let's explore more about scenarios where you can further power your development journey by utilizing prompt engineering to improve various aspects of the software development lifecycle, including code generation, documentation, debugging, testing, and learning new technologies.

Code Generation and Completion

Prompt engineering can significantly enhance the process of writing code.

Generating Code Snippets in Various Languages: Developers can use prompts to generate code snippets in different programming languages, saving time and effort.

Examples:

Prompt: "Generate a Python function that sorts a list of numbers in ascending order."

Output (Python):

```
def sort_ascending(numbers):
return sorted(numbers)
```

Prompt: "Write a JavaScript function to fetch data from an API and display it on a webpage." * Output:

JavaScript

```
async function fetchData(url) {
const response = await fetch(url);
```

```
const data = await response.json();
// Code to display data on webpage
}
```

Automating Repetitive Coding Tasks: Prompts can be used to automate repetitive coding tasks, such as generating boilerplate code or converting code from one format to another.

Examples:

Prompt: "Generate a class with getter and setter methods for the following attributes: name (string), age (integer), email (string)."

Output: (The LLM would generate the class with the specified methods)

Prompt: "Convert the following CSV data into a JSON array: [CSV Data]"

Output: (The LLM would provide the JSON equivalent of the CSV data)

Creating Code from Natural Language Descriptions: Developers can use natural language prompts to describe the functionality they want to implement, and the LLM can generate the corresponding code.

Examples:

Prompt: "Write a function that calculates the factorial of a given number."

Output (Python):

```
def factorial(n):
  if n == 0:
    return 1
  else:
    return n * factorial(n - 1)
```

Prompt: "Create a regular expression to validate email addresses." *

Output:

```
/^(([^<>()[\]\\.,;:\s@\"]+(\.[^<>()[
\]\\.,;:\s@\"]+)*)|(\".+\"))@((\[[0-
9]{1,3}\.[0-9]{1,3}\.[0-9]{1,3}\.[0-
9]{1,3}\])|(([a-zA-Z\-0-9]+\.)+[a-
zA-Z]{2,}))$/
```

Code Explanation and Documentation

Prompt engineering can also be used to improve code readability and maintainability. Generating Code Comments and Documentation

Prompts can help developers generate code comments and documentation, making it easier for others (and their future selves) to understand the code.

Examples:

Prompt: "Generate comments for the following Python function: [Python Function]"

Output: (The LLM would add comments to explain the function's purpose, parameters, and return value)

Prompt: "Write a documentation string for the following JavaScript code: [JavaScript Code]"

Output: (The LLM would generate a documentation string that describes the code's functionality)

Explaining Complex Code Logic: Prompts can be used to explain complex code logic in plain language, making it more accessible to developers of all skill levels.

Examples:

Prompt: "Explain the following regular expression: `^[a-zA-Z]+$`"

Output: **"This regular expression matches a string that consists of one or more letters (both uppercase and lowercase) from the beginning to the end of the string."**

Prompt: "Describe the functionality of the following code snippet: [Code Snippet]"

Output: (The LLM would provide a clear and concise explanation of what the code does)

Translating Code Between Languages: Prompts can assist in translating code from one programming language to another, which can be useful when migrating codebases or working with different technologies.

Examples:

Prompt: "Translate the following Python code to JavaScript: [Python Code]"

Output: (The LLM would provide the JavaScript equivalent of the Python code)

Prompt: "Convert the following Java code to C#: [Java Code]"

Output: (The LLM would provide the C# equivalent of the Java code)

Debugging and Code Review

Prompt engineering can also be a valuable tool for debugging code and performing code reviews.

Identifying and Fixing Bugs: Prompts can help developers identify and fix bugs in their code by analyzing error messages, stack traces, and code snippets.

Examples:

Prompt: "Analyze the following error message and suggest possible solutions: [Error Message]"

Output: (The LLM would provide potential causes of the error and suggest ways to fix it)

Prompt: "Identify any bugs in the following code snippet: [Code Snippet]"

Output: (The LLM would point out potential issues in the code)

Suggesting Code Improvements: Prompts can be used to suggest improvements to code, such as making it more efficient, readable, or maintainable.

Examples:

Prompt: "Suggest ways to optimize the following code for performance: [Code Snippet]"

Output: (The LLM would provide suggestions for improving the code's efficiency)

Prompt: "How can I make this code more readable and maintainable? [Code Snippet]"

Output: (The LLM would offer suggestions for improving the code's clarity and structure)

Automating Code Reviews: Prompts can assist in automating parts of the code review process, such as checking for coding style violations or identifying potential security vulnerabilities.

Examples:

Prompt: "Review the following code for adherence to coding style guidelines: [Code Snippet]"

Output: (The LLM would point out any style violations in the code)

Prompt: "Identify potential security vulnerabilities in the following code: [Code Snippet]"

Output: (The LLM would highlight any security risks in the code)

Testing and Quality Assurance

Prompt engineering can also play a role in software testing and quality assurance.

Generating Unit Tests and Integration Tests: Prompts can help developers generate unit tests and integration tests to ensure the quality of their code.

Examples:

Prompt: "Generate unit tests for the following Python function: [Python Function]"

Output: (The LLM would generate unit tests for the function using a testing framework like unit test)

Prompt: "Create integration tests for the following API endpoint: [API Endpoint]"

Output: (The LLM would generate integration tests to verify the API endpoint's functionality)

Creating Test Data: Prompts can be used to generate test data for various testing purposes, such as performance testing or security testing.

Examples:

Prompt: "Generate a set of realistic test data for a user registration form, including valid and invalid inputs."

Output: (The LLM would generate test data with various names, email addresses, passwords, etc.)

Prompt: "Create test data for performance testing a database query, with varying data volumes."

Output: (The LLM would generate datasets of different sizes to test the query's performance)

Analyzing Test Results: Prompts can assist in analyzing test results, identifying trends, and pinpointing the root cause of test failures.

Examples:

Prompt: "Analyze the following test results and identify any patterns or trends: [Test Results]"

Output: (The LLM would provide insights into the test results, such as which tests are failing most frequently)

Prompt: "Explain the cause of the following test failure: [Test Failure Log]"

Output: (The LLM would analyze the test failure log and explain why the test failed)

Learning and Exploring New Technologies

Prompt engineering can also be a valuable tool for developers who are learning new technologies.

Generating Tutorials and Examples: Prompts can help developers generate tutorials and examples to learn new programming languages, frameworks, or libraries.

Examples:

Prompt: "Generate a tutorial on how to use React hooks."

Output: (The LLM would provide a step-by-step tutorial with code examples)

Prompt: "Show me examples of how to use the map function in JavaScript."

Output: (The LLM would provide code examples demonstrating the usage of the map function)

Summarizing Technical Documentation: Prompts can be used to summarize technical documentation, making it easier for developers to find the information they need.

Examples:

Prompt: "Summarize the following documentation for the [Library Name] library: [Documentation Text]"

Output: (The LLM would provide a concise summary of the documentation)

Prompt: "Give me the key points from this article about [Technology]: [Article Text]"

Output: (The LLM would extract and summarize the most important information from the article)

Exploring Different Architectural Patterns: Prompts can assist developers in exploring different architectural patterns and understanding their trade-offs.

Examples:

Prompt: "Explain the microservices architectural pattern and it's advantages and disadvantages."

Output: (The LLM would provide an explanation of the pattern, along with it's pros and cons)

Prompt: "Compare and contrast the Model-View-Controller (MVC) and Model-View-ViewModel (MVVM) architectural patterns."

Output: (The LLM would provide a comparison of the two patterns)

The provided statement succinctly captures the core drivers behind the increasing adoption of prompt engineering by software developers. The potential to boost productivity, enhance code quality, cut costs, accelerate delivery, and foster learning paints a compelling picture of a future where AI-augmented development becomes the norm. As AI continues it's rapid evolution, the innovative applications of prompt engineering within software development are poised to expand dramatically, fundamentally reshaping how developers work and the software they create.

To fully appreciate the transformative impact of prompt engineering on developers, it is critical that you delve into each of these driving factors in detail and explore the practical implications for their daily workflows and skill sets.

Increased Productivity and Efficiency:

One of the most immediate and significant benefit's of prompt engineering for developers lies in it's potential to automate or streamline repetitive and time-consuming tasks. Instead of manually writing boilerplate code, generating test cases, or even debugging common errors, developers can leverage well-crafted prompts to instruct AI models to perform these activities.

For instance, a developer might use a prompt like: "Generate a Python function that connects to a PostgreSQL database and retrieves all records from the 'users' table." The AI can then generate the basic code structure, saving the developer valuable time and effort. Similarly, prompts can be used to generate unit tests for specific code modules, create documentation snippets, or even refactor existing code based on predefined style guides.

This automation frees up developers to focus on more complex problem-solving, architectural design, and the core logic of the application. By offloading routine tasks to AI assistants powered by prompt engineering, developers can achieve higher output with the same amount of effort, leading to significant gains in overall productivity and efficiency. This is particularly valuable in fast-paced development environments with tight deadlines.

Improved Code Quality and Maintainability:

Prompt engineering can contribute to higher code quality and improved maintainability in several ways. AI models trained on vast codebases and best practices can be prompted to generate code that adheres to established coding standards, follows consistent naming conventions, and incorporates error handling mechanisms.

For example, a developer could use a prompt like: "Generate a JavaScript function to validate an email address, ensuring it follows standard RFC 5322 format and includes appropriate error messages." The AI can produce code that is not only functional but also well-structured and easier to understand.

Furthermore, prompt engineering can assist in identifying potential code smells and suggesting refactoring strategies. By prompting an AI to analyze existing code for complexity, redundancy, or potential performance bottlenecks, developers can proactively address these issues, leading to a more robust and maintainable codebase in the long run. This proactive approach to quality can significantly reduce the accumulation of technical debt.

Reduced Development Costs:

The combined effects of increased productivity and improved code quality directly translate into reduced development costs. By automating tasks and minimizing errors, organizations can achieve more with fewer developer hours. Faster development cycles also contribute to cost savings by accelerating time to market and allowing for quicker realization of business value.

Moreover, the ability of prompt engineering to assist in areas like automated testing and early bug detection can significantly reduce the costs associated with fixing defects later in the development lifecycle, which are typically much more expensive to address. By catching issues early, organizations can avoid costly rework and ensure a more efficient use of development resources.

Accelerated Time to Market:

In today's competitive landscape, the ability to rapidly develop and deploy new features and applications is crucial. Prompt engineering can significantly accelerate the time to market by streamlining various stages of the development process.

The automation of code generation, testing, and documentation allows developers to move through development cycles more quickly. By reducing the time spent on routine tasks, developers can dedicate more effort to implementing core functionalities and delivering value to users faster. This agility can provide a significant competitive advantage.

Prompt engineering can also facilitate rapid prototyping and experimentation. Developers can use prompts to quickly generate basic versions of features or applications, allowing for early feedback and iteration, further accelerating the development process and ensuring that the final product aligns with user needs.

Enhanced Developer Learning and Knowledge Sharing:

Prompt engineering can also serve as a powerful tool for developer learning and knowledge sharing within teams. By interacting with AI models through prompts, developers can gain insights into different coding paradigms, best practices, and even learn new programming languages or frameworks.

For instance, a junior developer could prompt an AI: "Explain the concept of dependency injection in the context of Angular and provide a simple code example." The AI can provide a clear explanation and illustrative code, acting as a personalized learning resource.

Prompts and the resulting AI-generated code can serve as a basis for discussions and knowledge sharing within development teams. Reviewing and analyzing AI-generated code can spark conversations about different approaches and best practices, fostering a culture of continuous learning and improvement. This can be particularly beneficial for onboarding new team members or upskilling existing developers in new technologies.

Expanding Applications of Prompt Engineering for Developers:

Beyond these core drivers, the applications of prompt engineering for developers are continuously expanding as AI technology evolves. Some emerging and potential future applications include:

i. **AI-Powered Debugging**: Developers could use prompts to describe a bug and ask the AI to suggest potential causes and solutions or even generate code to automatically fix the issue.

ii. **Security Vulnerability Detection**: Prompting AI models to analyze code for common security vulnerabilities like SQL injection or cross-site scripting could lead to more secure applications.

iii. **Performance Optimization**: Developers could use prompts to identify performance bottlenecks in their code and receive suggestions for optimization techniques.

iv. **Cross-Platform Development Assistance**: AI could be prompted to generate code snippets or translate code between different platforms or languages.

v. **Generating Realistic Mock Data**: Developers can use prompts to create large and realistic datasets for testing and development purposes, saving significant time and effort in manual data creation.

vi. **Assisting with Architectural Design**: While still in its early stages, prompt engineering could potentially assist in generating architectural diagrams or suggesting design patterns based on project requirements.

vii. **Natural Language Interaction with Development Tools**: Imagine using natural language prompts to perform actions within an IDE, such as "Create a new branch named 'feature-x'" or "Run all unit tests in this directory."

Good to Remember:

i. **Specify the Task and Scope Clearly:** When prompting for code, explicitly state the desired functionality, the programming language, any relevant libraries or frameworks, and the scope of the code you need (e.g., a single function, a class, a module). For testing, define what aspects of the code need to be tested (e.g., functional behaviour, edge cases, performance). For test cases, specify the input conditions, expected outputs, and the testing framework.

ii. **Provide Context and Examples:** Include relevant code snippets, data structures, user stories, or existing test cases to give the AI tool a better understanding of the problem domain and expected behaviour. If you have a specific style or pattern, you want the AI to follow, providing a few-shot example within the prompt can be highly beneficial.

iii. **Break Down Complex Tasks:** For intricate coding or testing requirements, decompose the problem into smaller, more manageable prompts. Instead of asking for an entire feature implementation at once, prompt for individual functions or components. Similarly, for testing, prompt for test cases for specific unit's or functionalities before asking for end-to-end tests.

iv. **Iterate and Refine Your Prompts:** The first output from the AI might not always be perfect, no matter how mind-blowing it may seem. Treat it ONLY as a starting point. Review the generated code, tests, or test cases, and then refine your prompts based on the results. Provide feedback to the AI by highlighting what's good, what's wrong, and what needs to be adjusted. This iterative process is key to achieving the desired outcome.

v. **Focus on Clarity and Testability**: When prompting for code, emphasize the need for clear, readable, and testable code. Similarly, when prompting for test cases, specify that they should be comprehensive, cover various scenarios, and be easily executable by testing frameworks. This encourages the AI to generate outputs that are not only functional but also maintainable and verifiable.

In this chapter we explored prompt engineering for developers and it's increasing adoption: boosting productivity and efficiency by automating routine tasks, improving code quality and maintainability through AI-driven best practices, reducing development costs by accelerating timelines and minimizing errors, accelerating time to market by streamlining development cycles, and enhancing developer learning and knowledge sharing through AI-powered explanations and code examples.

Further, emerging applications like AI-powered debugging, security vulnerability detection, and performance optimization, painting a picture of an AI-augmented future for software development.

For developers to effectively leverage prompt engineering, it's important to master clear and specific prompting, critically evaluating and validating AI-generated code, understanding the limitations and biases of AI models, iteratively refining prompts based on feedback, and thoughtfully integrating prompt engineering into existing workflows as a tool to augment, not replace, human skills.

Chapter 7

Prompt Engineering for Agile Leaders

In the preceding chapters, we've explored the transformative power of prompt engineering across various Agile roles. So far, we have seen how Scrum Masters can leverage AI to facilitate events, enhance team collaboration, and streamline communication. Chapter 5 showcased Product Owners using prompts to refine product vision, manage backlogs, and deeply understand user needs. Finally, the previous chapter talked about how Developers can employ prompt engineering to boost coding efficiency, improve code quality, and accelerate learning.

This journey highlights a crucial evolution: prompt engineering isn't just a collection of techniques; it's a strategic capability that can reshape the entire Agile organization.

Now, we ascend to the leadership. The muscle force, the prime movers and as I love to call them, "*The people who put ink on the cheque*".

Agile leaders – be they executives, managers, or change agents – face unique challenges in guiding their organizations through complex transformations and fostering a culture of innovation. This chapter will reveal how prompt engineering can empower these leaders to navigate uncertainty, make data-driven decisions, and cultivate an AI-ready Agile enterprise.

Why is this chapter important?

Today, businesses around the world are dynamic than ever before. Agile leaders need to be more strategic, data-driven, and adaptable than ever before. Doing what you were doing so far, isn't going to take you places anymore.

I once saw a poster on my colleague's desk "Run faster than Yesterday to remain at the same spot Today". This is the harsh reality, you like it or not.

Prompt engineering is no magic, as you read this many leaders are already harnessing the power of prompting at their desks world-wide. Doing it in a better, structured fashion only helps them with a powerful set of tools to:

- **Gain deeper insights from complex data:** LLMs can analyze vast amounts of information and extract key trends and patterns.

- **Make more informed decisions:** AI can help leaders evaluate different options and predict potential outcomes.
- **Drive organizational change:** Prompt engineering can facilitate communication, training, and knowledge sharing.
- **Foster a culture of innovation:** AI can assist in brainstorming new ideas and evaluating their feasibility.

The modern business landscape is characterized by relentless change, demanding agility, and the constant pursuit of competitive advantage. C-suite executives, business leaders, decision-makers, and agile leaders bear the weighty responsibility of navigating this complexity, charting strategic courses, and empowering their organizations to thrive.

Traditionally, their roles have been defined by strategic planning, financial oversight, risk management, talent development, and fostering a culture of innovation and adaptation. However, the advent of Generative AI, particularly when harnessed through the nuanced art of Prompt Engineering, presents a paradigm shift, offering unprecedented capabilities to augment their decision-making, enhance their strategic foresight, and optimize their operational efficiency.

This chapter delves into the traditional responsibilities of these leadership roles and meticulously explores how Generative AI, powered by thoughtfully crafted prompts, can revolutionize their day-to-day activities, providing insights, automating analysis, and unlocking new avenues for strategic action.

The Evolving Role of the C-Suite Executive

Traditionally, C-suite executives (CEOs, CFOs, COOs, CMOs, CTOs, etc.) are the architects of organizational vision and strategy. They are responsible for setting the overall direction of the company, ensuring financial health, optimizing operations, driving market growth, leveraging technology, and cultivating a high-performing culture. Their days are often filled with strategic meetings, financial reviews, stakeholder communications, risk assessments, and crucial decisions that shape the future of the enterprise.

Let's see how Generative AI with Prompt Engineering Can Empower C-Suite Executives?

i. **Enhanced Strategic Foresight and Scenario Planning**: C-suite executives are tasked with anticipating future trends and formulating robust strategies. Generative AI can analyze vast datasets – market reports, economic indicators, competitor activities, technological advancements – and, guided by specific prompts, generate potential future scenarios and their implications.

For instance, a CEO could use prompts to explore the long-term impact of emerging technologies on their industry or to model the potential outcomes of different market entry strategies. This enables more informed strategic planning and proactive risk mitigation.

ii. **Deeper Market and Competitive Intelligence**: Understanding the competitive landscape is paramount. Generative AI can sift through news articles, social media, financial reports, and industry publications, and, when prompted effectively, synthesize comprehensive competitive analyzes, identify emerging threats and opportunities, and even predict competitor moves. A CMO could use prompts to understand competitor marketing campaigns' effectiveness or to identify unmet customer needs that competitors are failing to address.

iii. **Improved Stakeholder Communication and Engagement**: C-suite executives spend considerable time communicating with various stakeholders – investors, employees, customers, and the board of directors. Generative AI can assist in crafting compelling narratives, tailoring messages to specific audiences, and even anticipating potential stakeholder concerns based on past interactions and sentiment analysis of public data. A CEO preparing for an investor call could use prompts to generate talking points that address key investor concerns and highlight future growth prospects.

iv. **Data-Driven Financial Analysis and Forecasting**: CFOs are responsible for the financial health of the organization. Generative AI can analyze complex financial data, identify trends, generate insightful reports, and create more accurate financial forecasts based on various economic and business variables, guided by specific prompts. A CFO could use prompts to analyze the impact of different investment scenarios on the company's profitability or to identify potential areas for cost optimization.

v. **Optimized Operational Efficiency and Risk Management**: COOs are focused on streamlining operations and managing risks. Generative AI can analyze operational data, identify bottlenecks, predict potential disruptions in the supply chain, and even suggest optimization strategies based on specific prompts. A COO could use prompts to analyze production efficiency data and identify areas for improvement or to assess the potential impact of geopolitical events on the supply chain.

vi. **Personalized Leadership and Talent Development**: Even at the highest level, understanding and nurturing talent is crucial. Generative AI can analyze employee performance data, identify skill gaps, and, guided by prompts, suggest personalized development plans or identify potential future leaders within the organization. A CEO could use prompts to understand employee sentiment across different departments or to identify individuals with high potential for specific leadership roles.

vii. **Empowering Business Leaders and Decision Makers**: Business leaders and decision-makers, operating at various levels within the organization, are responsible for translating the overarching strategy into actionable plans and making critical choices that impact their respective domains. Their traditional roles involve analyzing data, evaluating options, collaborating with teams, and driving execution.

viii. **Accelerated Data Analysis and Insight Generation**: Business leaders often need quick access to relevant insights from vast amounts of data. Generative AI can analyze reports, spreadsheets, and other data sources, and, when prompted effectively, summarize key findings, identify correlations, and generate actionable insights in a fraction of the time it would take traditional methods. A marketing manager could use prompts to quickly understand the performance of different marketing campaigns or to identify key customer segments driving sales growth.

ix. **More Informed Resource Allocation and Budgeting**: Making sound decisions about resource allocation is critical. Generative AI can analyze historical data, project future needs, and, guided by specific prompts, suggest optimal resource allocation strategies and assist in budget planning. A department head could use prompts to justify budget requests based on projected ROI and alignment with strategic goals.

x. **Risk Assessment and Mitigation Strategies**: Identifying and mitigating risks is a key responsibility. Generative AI can analyze internal and external data to identify potential risks and, when prompted effectively, suggest mitigation strategies and assess their potential effectiveness. A compliance officer could use prompts to identify emerging regulatory risks relevant to the organization's operations.

xi. **Revolutionizing Agile Leadership:** Agile leaders, including Scrum Masters, Product Owners, and Agile Coaches, focus on facilitating iterative development, fostering collaboration, and ensuring the delivery of value. Their traditional roles involve facilitating ceremonies, removing impediments, coaching teams, and working closely with stakeholders to define and prioritize the product backlog.

Now, let us have a closer look at scenarios where Agile Leaders are leveraging Prompt Engineering:

Strategic Planning and Visioning

Agile leaders are responsible for setting the strategic direction of their organizations. Prompt engineering can assist in this process by providing insights, generating options, and crafting compelling visions.

Analyzing Market Trends and Competitive Landscapes

Prompts can help leaders analyze market data, identify emerging trends, and assess the competitive landscape.

Example 1:

Prompt: "Analyze the following market research report on the electric vehicle industry and identify the key growth drivers and potential challenges: [Market Research Report]"

Output: **"Key growth drivers: Increasing environmental awareness, government incentives, technological advancements in battery technology. Potential challenges: High battery costs, limited charging infrastructure, competition from traditional automakers."**

Example 2:

Prompt: "Compare and contrast the business strategies of the following three competitors in the cloud computing market: [Competitor A Strategy], [Competitor B Strategy], [Competitor C Strategy]"

Output: **"Competitor A: Focuses on providing a wide range of services at a competitive price. Competitor B: Emphasizes innovation and cutting-edge technologies. Competitor C: Targets specific industry verticals with tailored solutions."**

Example 3:

Prompt: "Identify potential disruptive technologies that could impact the future of the retail industry."

Output: **"Potential disruptive technologies: Augmented reality (AR) for virtual try-on experiences, blockchain for supply chain transparency, and AI-powered personalized recommendations."**

Generating Strategic Options and Scenarios

Prompts can help leaders explore different strategic options and generate various scenarios for the future.

Example 1:

Prompt: "Generate three potential growth strategies for a software company that wants to expand its market share."

Output: **"1. Develop new products for adjacent markets. 2. Acquire smaller competitors to increase market share. 3. Form strategic partnerships to reach new customers."**

Example 2:

Prompt: "Create three different scenarios for the future of the global economy over the next 5 years, considering factors such as inflation, interest rates, and geopolitical events."

Output: **"Scenario 1: Continued economic growth with moderate inflation. Scenario 2: Global recession due to rising interest rates. Scenario 3: Economic instability caused by geopolitical conflicts."**

Example 3:

Prompt: "Brainstorm innovative ways to improve customer retention for a subscription-based service."

Output: **"Personalized onboarding experiences, proactive customer support, loyalty programs, and exclusive content for long-term subscribers."**

Crafting Compelling Vision Statements

Prompts can assist leaders in crafting compelling vision statements that inspire and motivate their organizations.

Example 1:

Prompt: "Write a vision statement for a healthcare company that aims to improve the quality of life for patients."

Output: **"To create a world where everyone has access to personalized, proactive, and compassionate healthcare, empowering individuals to live healthier and more fulfilling lives."**

Example 2:

Prompt: "Generate an inspiring vision statement for an organization focused on space exploration."

Output: **"To pioneer the future of humanity by expanding our reach beyond Earth, unlocking the mysteries of the universe, and creating a sustainable future among the stars."**

Example 3:

Prompt: "Craft a concise and impactful vision statement for a non-profit dedicated to environmental conservation."

Output: **"A healthy planet for thriving communities."**

Decision Support and Insights

Agile leaders need to make informed decisions based on data and insights. Prompt engineering can help them extract valuable information, identify risks and opportunities, and forecast future outcomes.

Extracting Key Insights from Data

Prompts can help leaders analyze data from various sources and extract key insights that can inform their decisions.

Example 1:

Prompt: "Analyze the following customer feedback data and identify the top 3 customer pain points: [Customer Feedback Data]"

Output: **"Top 3 customer pain points: 1. Slow website loading speed. 2. Difficulty finding products. 3. Lack of responsive customer support."**

Example 2:

Prompt: "Extract the key financial metrics from the following quarterly report: [Quarterly Report]"

Output: **"Key financial metrics: Revenue growth: 15%, Net profit margin: 10%, Customer acquisition cost: $20."**

Example 3:

Prompt: "Summarize the findings of this employee engagement survey, highlighting areas of strength and areas for improvement: [Employee Engagement Survey Data]"

Output: **"Strengths: High levels of teamwork and collaboration. Areas for improvement: Need for more career development opportunities and better communication from management."**

Identifying Risks and Opportunities

Prompts can help leaders identify potential risks and opportunities that could impact their organizations.

Example 1:

Prompt: "Identify potential risks associated with launching a new product in a highly competitive market."

Output: **"Potential risks: Price wars with competitors, lack of product differentiation, negative customer reviews, and slower-than-expected adoption rates."**

Example 2:

Prompt: "What are the potential opportunities for our company to leverage artificial intelligence to improve our operations?"

Output: **"Opportunities: Automating customer service interactions, personalizing marketing campaigns, optimizing supply chain management, and developing AI-powered products."**

Example 3:

Prompt: "Analyze the current economic climate and identify potential threats and opportunities for the real estate market."

Output: **"Threats: Rising interest rates, inflation, and potential recession. Opportunities: Increased demand for sustainable housing and the growth of remote work leading to shifts in housing preferences."**

Forecasting Future Outcomes

Prompts can help leaders forecast future outcomes based on current trends and data.

Example 1:

Prompt: "Forecast the demand for our product over the next year, considering factors such as seasonality, economic growth, and competitor activity: [Historical Sales Data], [Market Trends]"

Output: "(The LLM would provide a forecast with estimated sales figures for each quarter)"

Example 2:

Prompt: "Predict the potential impact of climate change on our supply chain over the next 10 years."

Output: "(The LLM would analyze potential disruptions due to extreme weather events, resource scarcity, and regulatory changes)"

Example 3:

Prompt: "Based on current trends, what is the projected growth of the renewable energy sector in the next decade?"

Output: "(The LLM would provide a forecast for market size, investment, and technology adoption rates in the renewable energy sector)"

Organizational Change and Transformation

Agile leaders often need to guide their organizations through significant change and transformation. Prompt engineering can facilitate this process by improving communication, generating training materials, and fostering organizational learning.

Communicating Change Initiatives

Prompts can help leaders craft clear, concise, and compelling messages to communicate change initiatives to their employees.

Example 1:

Prompt: "Write an email to employees announcing a new organizational restructuring, explaining the reasons for the change and its potential benefits."

Output: "(The LLM would generate an email with a clear and positive message, addressing employee concerns and highlighting the benefits of the restructuring)"

Example 2:

Prompt: "Develop a communication plan for introducing a new Agile methodology to the development teams."

Output: "(The LLM would outline a plan with key messages, communication channels, and a timeline for introducing Agile practices)"

Example 3:

Prompt: "Create talking points for a town hall meeting where the CEO will address employee concerns about the company's shift to remote work."

Output: "(The LLM would generate talking points that address common concerns about productivity, communication, and work-life balance in a remote work environment)"

Generating Training Materials

Prompts can assist in creating training materials, such as presentations, guides, and tutorials, to help employees adapt to new processes, technologies, or roles.

Example 1:

Prompt: "Generate a training module on how to use a new software application."

Output: "(The LLM would create a training module with step-by-step instructions, screenshots, and exercises)"

Example 2:

Prompt: "Develop a training program for managers on how to lead Agile teams."

Output: "(The LLM would outline a training program with topics such as Agile principles, Scrum framework, and servant leadership)"

Example 3:

Prompt: "Create a series of microlearning videos to teach employees about cybersecurity best practices."

Output: "(The LLM would generate outlines and scripts for short, engaging videos covering topics like password security, phishing awareness, and data protection)"

Facilitating Organizational Learning

Prompts can help leaders foster a culture of organizational learning by summarizing knowledge, generating FAQs, and creating knowledge bases.

Example 1:

Prompt: "Summarize the key learnings from a recent project and create a document to share them with other teams."

Output: "(The LLM would generate a document summarizing the project's successes, challenges, and lessons learned)"

Example 2:

Prompt: "Generate a FAQ document to address common questions about a new company policy."

Output: "(The LLM would create a FAQ document with clear and concise answers to frequently asked questions)"

Example 3:

Prompt: "Develop a framework for creating a company-wide knowledge base, including guidelines for content creation, organization, and maintenance."

Output: "(The LLM would outline a structure and set of guidelines for building a comprehensive and accessible knowledge base)"

Innovation and Experimentation

Agile leaders are responsible for fostering a culture of innovation and experimentation. Prompt engineering can help them brainstorm new ideas, evaluate their feasibility, and create proposals.

Brainstorming New Ideas

Prompts can help leaders generate a wide range of innovative ideas for new products, services, or business models.

Example 1:

Prompt: "Brainstorm new product ideas for a company that specializes in sustainable packaging."

Output: **"Ideas: Biodegradable packaging made from seaweed, edible packaging, smart packaging with sensors to track product freshness."**

Example 2:

Prompt: "Generate innovative ways to improve the customer experience in a retail store."

Output: "Ideas: Personalized shopping recommendations through AR, contactless payment options, interactive displays that provide product information."

Example 3:

Prompt: "Brainstorm new business models for the music industry in the age of streaming."

Output: **"Ideas: Personalized music subscriptions based on mood and activity, virtual concerts with interactive elements, and blockchain-based royalty distribution."**

Evaluating the Feasibility of New Projects

Prompts can help leaders assess the feasibility of new projects by analyzing potential costs, benefits, and risks.

Example 1:

Prompt: "Evaluate the feasibility of developing a new mobile app, considering factors such as development costs, market demand, and competition."

Output: "(The LLM would provide an analysis of the project's feasibility, including potential challenges and opportunities)"

Example 2:

Prompt: "Assess the potential return on investment (ROI) for implementing a new CRM system, considering factors such as increased sales, improved customer satisfaction, and reduced operational costs."

Output: "(The LLM would provide an estimated ROI based on the provided data and assumptions)"

Example 3:

Prompt: "Analyze the ethical implications of using AI-powered facial recognition technology for security purposes."

Output: "(The LLM would discuss ethical concerns related to privacy, bias, and potential misuse of the technology)"

Creating Proposals and Business Cases

Prompts can assist in creating persuasive proposals and business cases to secure funding and support for new initiatives.

Example 1:

Prompt: "Write a proposal to secure funding for a new research and development project."

Output: "(The LLM would generate a proposal outlining the project's objectives, methodology, budget, and expected outcomes)"

Example 2:

Prompt: "Develop a business case for investing in a new marketing campaign, including an analysis of the target audience, marketing channels, and projected return on investment."

Output: "(The LLM would create a business case with a clear justification for the investment)"

Example 3:

Prompt: "Create a presentation to pitch a new product idea to potential investors, highlighting its unique value proposition and market opportunity."

Output: "(The LLM would generate a presentation outline and key talking points to effectively communicate the product's potential)"

Building an AI-Ready Agile Organization

Agile leaders play a crucial role in preparing their organizations for the age of AI. Prompt engineering can help them develop AI adoption strategies, promote a culture of experimentation, and address ethical considerations.

Developing AI Adoption Strategies

Prompts can help leaders develop comprehensive AI adoption strategies that align with their organizational goals.

Example 1:

Prompt: "Develop an AI adoption strategy for a manufacturing company, focusing on improving efficiency and reducing costs."

Output: "(The LLM would outline a strategy with key initiatives, such as implementing AI-powered predictive maintenance and optimizing supply chain management)"

Example 2:

Prompt: "Create a roadmap for integrating AI into the customer service department to enhance customer experience."

Output: "(The LLM would generate a roadmap with steps for implementing AI-powered chatbots, personalized recommendations, and sentiment analysis)"

Example 3:

Prompt: "Outline a plan for upskilling the workforce to effectively collaborate with AI tools and technologies."

Output: "(The LLM would propose training programs, workshops, and mentorship initiatives to prepare employees for an AI-driven environment)"

Promoting a Culture of Experimentation

Prompts can help leaders foster a culture of experimentation by encouraging employees to explore new ideas and try out different approaches.

Example 1:

Prompt: "Develop a set of guidelines for conducting experiments with AI tools and technologies."

Output: "(The LLM would create guidelines covering experiment design, data collection, analysis, and reporting)"

Example 2:

Prompt: "Design a program to incentivize employees to come up with innovative AI-related ideas."

Output: "(The LLM would suggest ideas such as hackathons, innovation challenges, and recognition programs)"

Example 3:

Prompt: "Create a communication strategy to encourage employees to share their learnings and best practices from AI experiments."

Output: "(The LLM would outline a plan for using internal communication channels to promote knowledge sharing and collaboration)"

Addressing Ethical Considerations

Prompts can help leaders address the ethical considerations associated with AI, such as bias, fairness, transparency, and accountability.

Example 1:

Prompt: "Identify potential ethical risks associated with using AI in hiring decisions and suggest mitigation strategies."

Output: "(The LLM would discuss risks such as bias in algorithms and lack of transparency, and propose strategies like auditing algorithms and ensuring human oversight)"

Example 2:

Prompt: "Develop a set of ethical principles for the development and deployment of AI systems within the organization."

Output: "(The LLM would generate a set of principles focusing on fairness, accountability, privacy, and security)"

Generative AI, powered by the precision and nuance of Prompt Engineering, offers a profound opportunity for C-suite executives, business leaders, decision-makers, and agile leaders to transcend the limitations of traditional analysis and decision-making processes. By learning to effectively communicate their needs and objectives through well-crafted prompts, leaders can unlock the immense potential of AI to gain deeper insights, make more informed decisions, optimize operations, and ultimately drive greater organizational success.

This is not about replacing human leadership but about augmenting it with intelligent assistance, enabling leaders to focus on strategic vision, foster innovation, and navigate the complexities of the modern business world with unprecedented clarity and foresight.

The future of effective leadership lies in embracing and mastering the art of leading the AI-powered enterprise through the strategic application of Prompt Engineering.

This concludes the second Part of this book.

If you are a relatively new Scrum Master, Product Owner or Developer, reading this far should be good enough for you to embark on the wave of Generative AI and leverage the most powerful techniques of Prompt Engineering and supercharge your everyday work.

However, chances are that you are reading this book to enhance your already good skills on prompting and wanting to take it to the next level.

We got you covered!

From now on, we are getting into some advanced topics of prompt engineering which individuals and organizations to get rid of the mundane repetitive tasks and make more cerebral room for innovation and thought leadership.

Part 3

Advanced Prompt Engineering

Chapter 8

Advanced Prompting Techniques For Agile:

If you have reach thus far, you are now equipped with a robust understanding of core prompt engineering principles and their application across various Agile roles. We've witnessed how well-crafted prompts can enhance communication, automate tasks, and drive strategic decision-making. However, as Agile methodologies tackle increasingly complex challenges and as Large Language Models (LLMs) evolve, we must venture beyond the fundamentals.

This chapter marks the beginning of the book's final section, "Advanced Prompt Engineering in Agile," and introduces cutting-edge techniques that unlock even greater potential.

Advanced prompting techniques are crucial for several reasons:

Handling Complexity: Agile teams often face intricate problems that require deep reasoning, planning, and multi-step solutions. Advanced techniques enable LLMs to tackle these challenges effectively.

Improving Reliability: Ensuring the consistency and accuracy of LLM outputs is paramount, especially in critical Agile contexts. Advanced techniques help to enhance the reliability of AI-generated results.

Enabling Agentic AI: The emergence of "Agentic AI," where LLMs can autonomously interact with their environment and take actions, opens up new possibilities for Agile automation. Techniques like ReAct are essential for building effective Agile agents.

This chapter lays the groundwork for understanding and utilizing these advanced techniques, paving the way for a future where Agile teams and AI agents work seamlessly together.

Refining Prompts for Specific Agile Contexts

This section emphasizes the importance of tailoring prompts to the nuances of different Agile situations.

Contextual Precision: The more specific the prompt is to the Agile context (e.g., a specific ceremony, a particular type of task), the better the LLM's output will be.

Example 1:

- **Generic Prompt:** "Generate some [*Agile tasks*]."
- **Refined Prompt:** "Generate a list of detailed subtasks for a developer to implement the

user story 'As a user, I want to be able to filter search results by date' within a two-day sprint."

Example 2:

- **Generic Prompt:** "Give me feedback on this [*Agile process*]."
- **Refined Prompt:** "Provide constructive feedback on our team's current approach to backlog refinement, focusing on how well we estimate story points and ensure stories are ready for development."

Example 3:

- **Generic Prompt:** "Write some meeting notes."
- **Refined Prompt:** "Generate concise meeting notes from this Sprint Retrospective, categorizing action items, positive feedback, and areas for improvement."
- **Role-Aware Prompting:** Explicitly define the roles involved in the Agile scenario to guide the LLM's perspective.

Example 1:

Generic Prompt: "What should we do about this [*user story*]?"

Refined Prompt: "As a Product Owner, analyze the following user story and provide three options for how to handle it, considering its business value and technical complexity."

Example 2:

Generic Prompt: "Give me some test cases for this [*problem*]."

Refined Prompt: "As a QA engineer, generate five test cases, including edge cases, for the following acceptance criteria of this user story: [Acceptance Criteria]"

Example 3:

Generic Prompt: "How can we improve as a Scrum Team?"

Refined Prompt: "Acting as an Agile coach, review these Sprint Retrospective notes and suggest three specific, actionable steps the development team can take to improve their code review process."

Constraint-Based Prompting: Include specific constraints or limitations relevant to the Agile context.

Example 1:

Generic Prompt: "Design a user interface."

Refined Prompt: "Design a user interface for a mobile application that allows users to track their daily water intake, adhering to Material Design principles and prioritizing ease of use."

Example 2:

Generic Prompt: "Write some code."

Refined Prompt: "Write a Python function to calculate the Fibonacci sequence, optimizing for memory efficiency and adhering to PEP 8 style guidelines."

Example 3:

Generic Prompt: "Plan a sprint."

Refined Prompt: "Plan a two-week sprint for a team of five developers, considering their skill sets and the dependencies between the following user stories: [List of User Stories]."

Combining Prompting Techniques for Complex Scenarios

Many real-world Agile situations require combining multiple prompting techniques to achieve the desired outcome.

Chain of Thought + Few-Shot: Use Chain of Thought prompting (CoT) to encourage the LLM to reason step-by-step and combine it with few-shot examples to guide the reasoning process.

Example 1:

Prompt: "Here are some examples of how to break down a complex user story into smaller tasks and estimate the effort for each task, showing your reasoning: [Few-Shot Examples of User Story Breakdown and Estimation]. Now, break down and estimate the user story 'As a user, I want to be able to generate a report of my sales data for the past year' into tasks."

Example 2:

Prompt: "I'll give you examples of how to analyze user feedback from a retrospective and identify actionable improvements, showing your reasoning: [Few-Shot Examples of Retrospective Analysis]. Now, analyze this feedback and suggest three concrete actions."

Example 3:

Prompt: "I'll provide examples of how to design an A/B test and explain the rationale behind each design choice: [Few-Shot Examples of A/B Test Design]. Design an A/B test to see if changing the button colour increases click-through rates."

Role Prompting + System Prompting: Combine role prompting to assign a persona to the LLM and system prompting to set the overall context and instructions.

Example 1:

Prompt: "You are an experienced Agile coach. Your task is to review the following Scrum team's process and provide recommendations. The team has been struggling with sprint planning. System prompt: Focus on identifying inefficiencies in their planning meetings and suggest practical improvements."

Example 2:

Prompt: "You are a software architect. Your task is to evaluate the following code for scalability and maintainability. System prompt: Consider best practices for microservices architecture and identify potential bottlenecks."

Example 3:

Prompt: "You are a UX researcher. Your task is to analyze the following user interview transcripts and summarize key user needs. System prompt: Prioritize insights that can inform the design of a new mobile application."

Contextual Prompting + Constraint-Based Prompting: Use contextual prompting to provide specific information about the Agile scenario and constraint-based prompting to guide the LLM within certain limitations.

Example 1:

Prompt: "Context: We are developing a feature for an e-commerce website. Constraint: The feature must be implemented within the current sprint (1 week). Design a user interface for a product comparison feature."

Example 2:

Prompt: "Context: We are writing documentation for a new API. Constraint: The documentation must be clear, concise, and targeted at developers with intermediate experience. Generate sample code snippets for common API calls."

Example 3:

Prompt: "Context: We are planning a release for a mobile application. Constraint: The release must be completed within the next two months. Create a release plan outlining the key features, milestones, and dependencies."

Self-Consistency in Agile Outputs

Self-consistency is a technique that enhances the reliability of LLM outputs by generating multiple responses to the same prompt and selecting the most consistent one. LLMs can sometimes produce inconsistent or contradictory outputs. Self-consistency mitigates this by leveraging the wisdom of the "crowd" of LLM-generated responses.

Example 1:

- Prompt: "Identify the top 3 risks for this project."
- Process: Generate 5 different lists of risks. Select the 3 risks that appear most frequently across the lists.

Example 2:

- Prompt: "Write an acceptance criterion for this user story: 'As a user, I want to be able to export my data.'"
- Process: Generate 8 different acceptance criteria. Choose the criterion that has the most common elements or the most similar phrasing across the generated outputs.

Application for Agile Teams:

Self-consistency can be particularly valuable for tasks where accuracy and reliability are critical, such as:

- Validating story points (based on pre-trained data)
- Identifying risks

- Defining acceptance criteria
- Prioritizing backlog items

Implementation Notes:

The number of samples (i.e., the number of LLM-generated responses) can be adjusted based on the desired level of accuracy and computational cost.

Methods for measuring consistency can vary (e.g., majority voting, similarity metrics).

Tree of Thoughts (ToT) for Agile Problem Solving

Tree of Thoughts (ToT) is a technique that extends Chain of Thought (CoT) by allowing the LLM to explore multiple reasoning paths and evaluate different options before arriving at a final answer.

While CoT encourages step-by-step reasoning, it follows a linear path. ToT enables more complex problem-solving by considering a "tree" of different thought sequences.

Example 1:

- Prompt: "Design a sprint plan for the following user stories, considering dependencies and team capacity."

- ToT Process:
    - LLM generates multiple possible first steps (e.g., "Prioritize user stories by business value," "Identify technical dependencies").
    - For each first step, the LLM generates multiple possible next steps.
    - The LLM evaluates the intermediate "thoughts" and prunes less promising branches.
    - This process continues until the LLM arrives at the most optimal sprint plan.

Example 2:

- Prompt: "What are the possible solutions to this production bug and what are the pros and cons of each solution?"
- ToT Process:
    - LLM generates multiple possible causes of the bug.
    - For each cause, it generates multiple possible solutions.
    - It then evaluates the solutions based on factors like implementation complexity, time to fix, and potential impact.

Example 3:

- Prompt: "How can we improve team collaboration during remote work?"
- ToT Process:
    - LLM generates different strategies like improving communication, using better tools, or fostering a stronger team culture.
    - It then expands on each strategy with specific tactics and considers the potential benefits and drawbacks of each.

Application for Agile Teams:

ToT is particularly useful for complex Agile tasks that involve:

- Planning and decision-making
- Problem-solving
- Design and optimization

Implementation Notes:

ToT requires more computational resources than CoT.

Effective evaluation and pruning of thought branches are crucial for ToT's success.

ReAct (Reasoning and Acting) for Agile Agents

ReAct (Reasoning and Acting) is a prompting technique that enhances the capabilities of Large Language Models (LLMs) to function as agents capable of interacting with their environment. It addresses limitations in traditional LLM prompting, which often struggles with tasks requiring a combination of logical inference and external information retrieval. ReAct enables LLMs to generate both reasoning traces and task-specific actions, allowing them to dynamically interact with external tools and systems to gather information and make decisions.

ReAct operates on the principle of interleaving reasoning and acting. Instead of solely generating text, the LLM produces a sequence of thoughts and actions. This allows the LLM to:

i. **Reason**: Generate intermediate thoughts to decompose the problem, track progress, and plan actions.
ii. **Act**: Interact with the environment by invoking external tools or systems (e.g., search engines, APIs, databases) to retrieve relevant information.

This interleaved process allows the LLM to adapt its reasoning based on the information it gathers through its actions, leading to more robust and accurate task completion.

Step-by-Step Approach to Using ReAct Prompting:

The following outlines a step-by-step approach to implementing ReAct prompting:

1. Define the Task and Environment:

i. Task Description: Clearly define the task the LLM agent needs to accomplish. This should be specific and measurable.

ii. Environment Setup: Identify the external tools or systems the agent can interact with. This might include:

   a. Search engines (e.g., Google Search API)

   b. APIs (e.g., retrieving data from a database, performing calculations)

   c. Knowledge bases (e.g., Wikipedia)

   d. Custom tools (e.g., internal systems)

iii. Tool Descriptions: Provide the LLM with descriptions of the available tools, including their functionality, input parameters, and expected output format. This is crucial for the LLM to understand how to use the tools effectively.

2. Design the ReAct Prompt Template:

The ReAct prompt template provides the LLM with the structure for generating interleaved thoughts and actions. It typically includes:

i. Task Description: A clear statement of the task.
ii. Tool Descriptions: Descriptions of the available tools.
iii. Example Demonstrations (Few-Shot Prompting): A few examples of successful task completion using the ReAct approach. These examples show the desired sequence of thoughts and actions.
iv. Current Input: The specific input for the current task instance.

```
Task: [Task Description]

Available Tools:
[Tool Descriptions]

Example 1:
Input: [Example Input 1]
Thought: [Reasoning step 1]
Action: [Action to take using a tool]
Observation: [Result from the tool]
Thought: [Reasoning step 2]
Action: [Action to take using a tool]
Observation: [Result from the tool]
Thought: [Final reasoning step]
Final Answer: [Answer to the task]

Example 2:
Input: [Example Input 2]
Thought: [Reasoning step 1]
Action: [Action to take using a tool]
Observation: [Result from the tool]
Thought: [Reasoning step 2]
Action: [Action to take using a tool]
Observation: [Result from the tool]
Thought: [Final reasoning step]
Final Answer: [Answer to the task]

Input: [Current Input]
```

Key Components of the Prompt Template Examples:

i. Input: The specific input for the task instance.

ii. Thought: A natural language sentence explaining the LLM's reasoning process. This might include:

   a. Decomposing the task into smaller steps.

   b. Identifying the information needed to proceed.

   c. Deciding which tool to use.

   d. Planning the next action.

   e. Synthesizing information from previous observations.

iii. Action: A structured call to a tool, specifying the tool name and input parameters. The action should be directly related to the current thought.

iv. Observation: The result returned by the tool after the action is executed. This is the LLM's view of the external world.

v. Final Answer: The LLM's final answer to the task, based on its reasoning and observations.

3. Iterate with the LLM:

i. Initial Prompt: Provide the LLM with the designed ReAct prompt template and the current input.
ii. LLM Response: The LLM generates a sequence of thoughts and actions.
iii. Execute Actions: Execute the actions specified by the LLM (i.e., call the external tools or systems).
iv. Provide Observations: Feed the results (observations) from the tool executions back to the LLM.
v. Continue Iteration: The LLM continues to generate thoughts and actions, incorporating the new observations, until it reaches a final answer or a predefined termination condition (e.g., maximum number of iterations).

4. Extract the Final Answer:

Once the LLM has generated a "Final Answer," extract this answer from the LLM's response. This is the result of the task.

Evaluate and Refine:

i. Evaluate Performance: Assess the performance of the ReAct agent on the given task. This might involve:

a. Measuring accuracy.

b. Analyzing the reasoning traces to identify errors.

c. Evaluating the efficiency of the tool usage.

ii. Refine Prompt: If the performance is not satisfactory, refine the ReAct prompt template. This might involve:

a. Adding more or different examples.

b. Modifying the wording of the task description or tool descriptions.

c. Adjusting the structure of the thought and action sequences in the examples.

iii. Iterate: Repeat steps 3-5 until the desired performance is achieved.

Detailed Explanation of Key Aspects of ReAct:

A. Reasoning (Thought Process):

The "Thought" component in ReAct is crucial for enabling the LLM to perform complex tasks. It allows the LLM to:

i. **Decompose Complex Tasks**: Break down a large task into smaller, more manageable sub-tasks. This makes the problem-solving process more structured and less prone to errors.

ii. **Track Progress**: Keep track of the current state of the task and the steps that have been taken. This helps the LLM to maintain context and avoid getting lost in the process.

iii. **Plan Actions**: Determine the most appropriate action to take based on the current state of the task and the available tools. This involves evaluating the potential outcomes of different actions and selecting the one that is most likely to lead to success.

iv. **Synthesize Information**: Combine information from previous observations to draw inferences and make decisions. This allows the LLM to learn from its interactions with the environment and adapt its behaviour accordingly.

v. **Handle Uncertainty**: Deal with situations where the available information is incomplete or ambiguous. The LLM can use its reasoning abilities to make educated guesses and explore different possibilities.

B. Acting (Tool Interaction):

The "Action" component enables the LLM to interact with the external world and gather information. This is essential for tasks that require accessing information beyond the LLM's internal knowledge.

i. **Tool Selection**: The LLM must select the appropriate tool to use based on the current information need. This requires understanding the functionality of each available tool and its relevance to the task at hand.

ii. **Parameter Specification**: The LLM must provide the correct input parameters for the selected tool. This requires understanding the input format and requirements of each tool.

iii. **Tool Execution**: The selected tool is executed with the specified parameters. This is typically handled by a separate component that interacts with the external systems.

iv. **Observation Retrieval**: The LLM receives the output from the tool as an "Observation." This observation provides the LLM with new information about the environment.

C. Interleaving Reasoning and Acting:

The key innovation of ReAct is the interleaving of "Thought" and "Action." This allows the LLM to:

i. **Adapt to New Information**: The LLM's reasoning is informed by the observations it receives from its actions. This allows it to dynamically adjust its strategy based on the information it gathers.

ii. **Explore the Environment**: The LLM can actively explore the environment by taking actions to gather more information. This is crucial for tasks where the required information is not readily available.

iii. **Overcome Limitations of LLMs:** LLMs have limitations in their ability to perform complex reasoning and access external information. ReAct helps to overcome these limitations by allowing the LLM to leverage external tools and systems.

iv. **Simulate Interactive Processes**: Many real-world tasks involve interacting with the environment in an iterative manner. ReAct allows LLMs to simulate these interactive processes, making them more suitable for real-world applications.

D. ReAct Prompt Engineering Considerations:

Effective ReAct prompting requires careful consideration of several factors:

i. **Clear Task Definition:** The task should be defined precisely and unambiguously. This helps the LLM to understand the goal and focus its reasoning and actions.

ii. **Comprehensive Tool Descriptions**: The descriptions of the available tools should be clear, concise, and accurate. This helps the LLM to understand how to use the tools effectively.

iii. **Relevant Examples:** The examples provided in the prompt template should be relevant to the task and demonstrate the desired sequence of thoughts and actions. The examples should cover a range of scenarios to help the LLM generalize.

iv. **Appropriate Level of Detail**: The level of detail in the thoughts and actions should be appropriate for the task. Too much detail can make the prompt verbose and difficult to understand, while too little detail can make it difficult for the LLM to reason effectively.

v. **Consistent Structure**: The structure of the prompt template should be consistent across all examples and the current input. This helps the LLM to learn the pattern and generate consistent outputs.

vi. **Iteration and Refinement**: Prompt engineering is an iterative process. It is important to evaluate the performance of the ReAct agent and refine the prompt template based on the results.

E. Advantages of ReAct:

Improved Accuracy: By allowing the LLM to gather information from external sources, ReAct can significantly improve the accuracy of its responses.

Enhanced Generalization: The ability to reason and act allows ReAct agents to generalize to new and unseen situations more effectively.

Increased Robustness: ReAct agents are more robust to errors and inconsistencies in the input, as they can use their reasoning abilities to identify and correct them.

Greater Flexibility: ReAct can be applied to a wide range of tasks that require both reasoning and action, making it a versatile technique for building LLM-powered agents.

F. Limitations of ReAct:

i. **Complexity**: Designing effective ReAct prompts can be complex and require careful consideration of the task, environment, and LLM capabilities.
ii. **Tool Dependence**: The performance of ReAct agents is heavily dependent on the availability and quality of the external tools.
iii. **Potential for Errors**: While ReAct improves robustness, LLMs can still make errors in their reasoning or action selection, especially in complex or ambiguous situations.
iv. **Computational Cost**: The iterative process of generating thoughts and actions can be computationally expensive.

ReAct represents a significant advancement in the development of LLM-powered agents. By enabling LLMs to reason and act, it opens up new possibilities for building intelligent systems that can interact with the world in a more dynamic and effective way. The step-by-step approach outlined above provides a practical guide for implementing ReAct prompting and leveraging its capabilities for a variety of tasks.

Here are some examples of using ReAct prompting:

Example 1:

Agile Agent Task: "Automatically schedule a Sprint Retrospective meeting with the team."

ReAct Process:

a. The LLM Reasons: "I need to find the team's availability and use a scheduling tool."

b. The LLM Acts: Uses a tool to check team members' calendars.

c. The LLM Reasons: "The best time is Friday at 3:00 PM. Now, I need to send out invitations."

d. The LLM Acts: Uses an email tool to send meeting invitations.

Example 2:

Agile Agent Task: "Monitor the team's communication channel and flag any potential blockers."

ReAct Process:

a. The LLM *Reasons*: "I need to access the team's chat history and identify keywords that indicate a blocker."
b. The LLM *Acts*: Accesses the chat history.
c. The LLM *Reasons*: "I found a message about an API integration issue. I should notify the relevant developer."
d. The LLM *Acts*: Sends a notification to the developer.

Example 3:

Agile Agent Task: "Update the sprint burndown chart based on task progress."

ReAct Process:

a. The LLM *Reasons*: "I need to retrieve the current task status and update the chart accordingly."
b. The LLM *Acts*: Accesses the task management system.
c. The LLM *Reasons*: "Task X is completed. I need to reduce the remaining work in the burndown chart."
d. The LLM *Acts*: Updates the sprint burndown chart.

Implementation Notes:

a. ReAct requires careful design of the LLM's "action space" (i.e., the set of tools and systems it can interact with).

b. Robust error handling and safety mechanisms are essential for ReAct agents.

Tools for ReAct Prompting: Beyond Basic LLMs

Implementing ReAct prompting effectively necessitates a toolkit that goes beyond simply using a free or readily available LLM. While LLMs are the core engine, the ReAct process involves orchestrating their interaction with external systems, managing the flow of information, and handling the execution of actions. This requires a combination of software development, API integration, and algorithmic control, which often demands coding and custom tool creation.

Why Regular Free LLM Tools May Not Suffice:

Basic, free LLM tools, often accessible through web interfaces or simple APIs, typically provide a limited and constrained environment. They are primarily designed for text generation and may lack the essential capabilities for ReAct implementation:

Limited State Management: ReAct requires maintaining the state of the agent's interaction, including the sequence of thoughts, actions, and observations. Free LLMs often operate in a stateless manner, making it difficult to track the conversation history and context necessary for ReAct.

No Tool Integration: ReAct relies on interacting with external tools (search engines, APIs, databases). Free LLMs rarely provide built-in mechanisms for connecting to and executing these tools.

Restricted Control Flow: ReAct involves a dynamic and iterative process of generating thoughts and actions based on observations. Free LLMs usually offer limited control over the generation process, making it challenging to implement the required logic.

Lack of Customization: ReAct often requires customizing the LLM's behaviour and response format. Free LLMs typically provide limited options for customizing the generation process or defining specific output structures.

Rate Limits and Usage Restrictions: Free LLM services often come with rate limits and usage restrictions, which can hinder the development and testing of ReAct agents that require frequent interactions.

Therefore, building a robust ReAct agent necessitates a more sophisticated approach, involving coding and the use of specialized tools and libraries.

Essential Tools and Technologies for ReAct Implementation:

The following tools and technologies are crucial for implementing ReAct prompting:

1. A Powerful and Flexible LLM API:

Choice of LLM: While free LLMs might be useful for initial experimentation, production-level ReAct applications often require access to more powerful and flexible LLMs, typically through paid APIs. Examples include:

OpenAI API: Provides access to GPT models with strong reasoning and code generation capabilities.

Google Cloud Vertex AI (*only an option, could be some other*): Offers access to PaLM 2 and other LLMs with advanced features.

Anthropic API: Provides access to Claude models, known for their strong conversational abilities.

API Access: Access to the LLM via an API is essential for programmatic interaction. This allows developers to send prompts, receive responses, and control the LLM's behaviour through code.

Customization Options: The LLM API should ideally provide options for customizing the generation process, such as:

Temperature: Controlling the randomness of the output.

Top-p sampling: Controlling the diversity of the output.

Maximum length: Limiting the length of the generated text.

Stop sequences: Defining sequences that indicate the end of the generation.

2. Programming Languages and Frameworks:

i. **Python**: Python is the most used programming language for working with LLMs and building ReAct agents. Its extensive libraries and frameworks make it well-suited for this task.

ii. **Libraries**: Several Python libraries are essential for ReAct implementation:

   a. **LangChain**: A framework specifically designed for developing LLM-powered applications. LangChain provides modules for prompt management, LLM interaction, tool integration, and agent orchestration, simplifying the ReAct process.

   b. **Requests**: A library for making HTTP requests to interact with APIs.

c. **JSON**: A library for working with JSON data, which is commonly used for communication with APIs.

d. **Regular expression libraries**: For parsing and extracting information from LLM responses.

iii. **Frameworks**: While not always strictly necessary, frameworks like Flask or FastAPI can be useful for building web applications or APIs that integrate ReAct agents.

3. Tool Integration Libraries and APIs:

ReAct agents need to interact with external tools and systems. This requires libraries and APIs for accessing these tools:

i. **Search Engine APIs:**

a. Google Search API (could be some other search providers as well): Provides access to Google Search results.

b. SerpAPI: Offers a unified API for accessing various search engines.

ii. **Knowledge Base APIs:**

a. **Wikipedia API**: Provides access to Wikipedia content.

b. **Database Libraries:**

i. psycopg2 (PostgreSQL): A Python library for connecting to PostgreSQL databases.
ii. mysql-connector-python (MySQL): A Python library for connecting to MySQL databases.
iii. sqlite3 (SQLite): A built-in Python library for working with SQLite databases.

iii. **Custom API Clients:** For interacting with custom or internal APIs, developers may need to create their own API clients using libraries like requests.

4. State Management Tools:

ReAct requires maintaining the state of the agent's interaction. This involves tracking the sequence of thoughts, actions, and observations.

i. **Dictionaries and Lists**: For simple ReAct implementations, Python dictionaries and lists can be used to store the conversation history.
ii. **Databases**: For more complex applications, databases (e.g., PostgreSQL, Redis) may be necessary to store and retrieve the agent's state persistently.

iii. **Caching Mechanisms**: Caching tools (e.g., Redis, Memcached) can be used to store frequently accessed information and improve performance.

5. Prompt Management Tools:

Managing and organizing prompts is crucial for ReAct development.

i. String Formatting: Python's string formatting capabilities (f-strings, .format()) can be used to create dynamic prompts.
ii. Template Engines: Template engines (e.g., Jinja2) can be used to create more complex and reusable prompt templates.
iii. LangChain's Prompt Templates: LangChain provides built-in support for managing and creating prompt templates, simplifying the process.

6. Logging and Debugging Tools:

Debugging ReAct agents can be challenging due to the complex interaction between the LLM and external tools.

i. **Python's logging Module**: For logging the agent's actions, thoughts, and observations.
ii. **Debugging Tools**: Python debuggers (e.g., pdb) can be used to step through the code and inspect the agent's state.

iii. **LLM API Logging**: Some LLM APIs provide logging capabilities that can be used to track the prompts sent and responses received.

7. Orchestration and Control Flow Logic:

The core of ReAct implementation lies in the code that orchestrates the interaction between the LLM and the tools. This involves:

i. **Coding the ReAct Loop**: Developers need to write code to implement the iterative loop that generates thoughts, executes actions, receives observations, and updates the LLM's context.

ii. **Handling Tool Execution**: The code needs to handle the execution of the selected tools, including making API calls, querying databases, or running external programs.

iii. **Parsing LLM Output**: The code needs to parse the LLM's output to extract the generated actions and determine the next step.

iv. **Managing Context**: The code needs to manage the conversation history and provide the LLM with the relevant context for each interaction.

v. **Error Handling**: Robust error handling needs to be implemented to deal with issues such as tool failures, API errors, or unexpected LLM responses.

Key ReAct Takeaways:

i. ReAct implementation necessitates coding and algorithmic control to manage the interaction between the LLM and external tools.

ii. Free LLM tools often lack the required features for state management, tool integration, and control flow.

iii. Developers need to use powerful LLM APIs, programming languages like Python, and specialized libraries like LangChain to build robust ReAct agents.

iv. Orchestrating the ReAct loop, handling tool execution, and parsing LLM output are crucial aspects of the implementation.

Alright people! You've journeyed through the wild and wonderful world of advanced prompt engineering, and it's time to gather 'round the campfire for a final, slightly bonkers, recap.

This ain't your grandma's recipe book summary, folks. We're talking pure, unadulterated, brain-tickling insights, delivered with a healthy dose of digital pizzazz.

So far, you've wrestled with the beast of complexity, and emerged, blinking, into the glorious dawn of AI-powered potential. So, grab your \popcorn, settle in, and let's recap the five most mind-bending, paradigm-shifting, jaw-dropping takeaways from our prompt engineering odyssey.

Good to Remember:

i. **Prompt Engineering**: It's Not Just Asking Nicely, It's an Art Form (and a Science, and a Little Bit of Magic): Forget "please" and "thank you." Advanced prompt engineering is about crafting intricate spells of language that coax, cajole, and command LLMs to dance to our tune. It's a delicate dance between precision and creativity, where a single word, a carefully placed comma, or a dash of metaphor can be the difference between AI brilliance and AI babble. We've learned that it's not just about what you say, but how you say it, with style, panache, and a healthy dose of strategic cunning. It's like being a digital Michelangelo, sculpting masterpieces of output from the raw clay of language. We're not just writing instructions; we're composing symphonies of semantics, conducting orchestras of code, and painting vibrant tapestries of text. So ditch the mundane requests and embrace the artistry of the prompt!

ii. **Context is King (and Queen, and the Entire Royal Court)**: Remember when your teachers droned on about context? Turns out, they were onto something (for once!). In the realm of advanced prompt engineering, context isn't just important; it's the entire freaking kingdom. We've discovered that LLMs are like super-smart, slightly forgetful, genies. You got to give them the whole backstory, the character motivations, the plot twists, and the emotional subtext, or they'll just grant you the most literal, and often hilariously useless, wish imaginable. We're not just asking questions; we're building entire worlds, complete with intricate backstories, detailed character arcs, and enough plot twists to make M. Night Shyamalan jealous. The more context you provide, the more coherent, relevant, and downright amazing the AI's response will be. So, don't be shy; unleash your inner storyteller and paint a vivid picture for your digital muse!

iii. **Iteration is Your BFF (Best Frenemy Forever)**: Forget the "one and done" approach. Advanced prompt engineering is a marathon, not a sprint. It's a delightful (and occasionally frustrating) dance of trial and error, a constant cycle of tweaking, refining, and experimenting. You craft a prompt, the LLM throws something back at you (sometimes brilliant, sometimes baffling), and you go back to the drawing board, armed with newfound knowledge and a slightly twitchy eye. We've learned that the best prompts are forged in the fires of iteration, honed by countless hours of experimentation, and polished to perfection through relentless refinement. It's like being a mad scientist, concocting ever-more-potent potions of language, each iteration bringing you closer to your ultimate goal. So, embrace the chaos, revel in the unexpected, and remember that every "failure" is just a stepping stone on the path to prompt perfection.

iv. **Tools, Tools, Glorious Tools (Because We're Not Doing This by Hand)**: While sheer linguistic prowess is admirable, advanced prompt engineering often requires a little help from our digital friends. We're talking about frameworks like LangChain, which act as our trusty sidekicks, providing the structure, the tools, and the sheer computational muscle to wrangle LLMs and orchestrate complex interactions. We've explored the power of vector databases for semantic search, the magic of chain-of-thought prompting for complex reasoning, and the sheer audacity of ReAct, which allows LLMs to not only think but also act upon the world. We're not just relying on our wit and charm; we're building elaborate contraptions of code and configuration, harnessing the full power of the digital realm to bend LLMs to our will. So, embrace the tools, master the frameworks, and become the ultimate prompt-wielding cyborg!

v. **The Ethics of AI**: Because We're Not Monsters (Hopefully): With great prompt power comes great responsibility. As we learn to wield these linguistic weapons with ever-greater skill, we must also grapple with the ethical implications of our creations. We've touched upon the dangers of bias, the potential for misuse, and the importance of transparency and accountability.

We're not just crafting clever prompts; we're shaping the future of AI, and we must do so with wisdom, foresight, and a healthy dose of moral compass calibration. We're not just building cool stuff; we're building the foundations of a new digital society, and we have a responsibility to ensure that this society is fair, just, and equitable for all. So, let's use our prompt powers for good, not evil, and strive to create AI that reflects the best of humanity, not the worst.

Now that you've moved beyond basic prompting to explore strategies for refining prompts with contextual precision, combining techniques for complex problem-solving, ensuring self-consistency for reliable outputs, and leveraging the groundbreaking potential of Tree of Thoughts and ReAct for sophisticated reasoning and autonomous agent behaviour. These methods are not merely incremental improvements; they represent a significant leap forward in our ability to harness AI to augment and even transform Agile practices.

The implications are profound. Imagine Agile teams empowered by AI agents that proactively manage workflows, resolve impediments, and optimize processes in real-time. Picture complex strategic decisions being navigated with the aid of LLMs that can explore a vast "tree" of potential outcomes.

The future we're glimpsing is one where the synergy between human ingenuity and AI capabilities reaches unprecedented levels, driving Agile to new heights of responsiveness and effectiveness.

In the next chapter, we'll embark on a new quest, a journey into the heart of prompt automation. We'll explore the techniques and technologies that allow us to automate the creation, management, and deployment of prompts, transforming prompt engineering from a manual, artisanal process into a streamlined, scalable, and downright efficient operation.

Chapter 9

Automating And Optimizing Prompts

We stand at the cusp of a new era in artificial intelligence, one where the power of Large Language Models (LLMs) is no longer confined to bespoke, handcrafted interactions, but is instead unleashed through the systematic application of automated and optimized prompting strategies. The preceding chapters have meticulously explored the art and science of prompt engineering, delving into the nuances of crafting effective instructions, harnessing advanced techniques, and navigating the ethical considerations that accompany this transformative technology. We have witnessed the evolution from basic requests to intricate linguistic architectures, capable of eliciting remarkable feats of reasoning, creativity, and action from these digital oracles.

However, the very success of prompt engineering in unlocking the potential of LLMs has exposed a critical bottleneck: the inherent limitations of manual, human-driven prompt creation and management. As the demand for LLM-powered applications explodes across industries and use cases, the traditional, artisanal approach to prompt crafting simply cannot scale to meet the burgeoning need. Imagine an organization seeking to integrate LLMs into every facet of its operations, from customer service and content creation to data analysis and strategic planning. The prospect of manually designing and maintaining thousands, or even tens of thousands, of unique prompts for each specific application becomes a logistical nightmare, a quagmire of complexity that threatens to stifle innovation and impede widespread adoption.

This is where the paradigm shift towards prompt automation and optimization becomes not merely desirable, but absolutely essential.

This chapter marks a critical transition, moving beyond the realm of individual prompt artistry and into the domain of scalable intelligence. We will explore the methodologies, tools, and best practices that empower organizations to automate the entire prompt lifecycle, from initial creation and refinement to dynamic management and continuous improvement. We will delve into the techniques that transform prompts from static instructions into dynamic, adaptive components of intelligent systems, capable of responding to evolving data, user needs, and business objectives.

The imperative for prompt automation stems from several fundamental challenges inherent in the manual approach:

The Scalability Challenge:

As LLM adoption expands, the sheer volume of prompts required to power diverse applications becomes overwhelming. Manually creating, managing, and updating prompts for each specific use case is a resource-intensive, time-consuming, and ultimately unsustainable endeavour. Organizations risk becoming bogged down in a prompt engineering bottleneck, where the creation and maintenance of prompts consume a disproportionate amount of human effort, hindering the pace of development and deployment. Automation provides the solution to this scalability challenge, enabling organizations to generate, deploy, and manage prompts at scale, without being constrained by the limitations of manual processes.

The Consistency and Reliability Challenge:

Manual prompt creation is inherently susceptible to human variability. Different prompt engineers may employ different styles, approaches, and levels of detail, leading to inconsistencies in prompt quality and effectiveness. This inconsistency can result in unpredictable LLM behaviour, making it difficult to ensure the reliability and accuracy of LLM-powered applications. Furthermore, as prompts are modified and updated over time, there is a risk of introducing errors or unintended consequences, further compromising the reliability of the system. Automation provides a framework for enforcing consistency and standardization in prompt design, ensuring that prompts are created and maintained according to predefined best practices, minimizing the risk of errors and maximizing the reliability of LLM outputs.

The Dynamic Adaptation Challenge:

The real world is a constantly evolving environment. User needs change, data distributions shift, and business objectives evolve. Prompts that were effective yesterday may become obsolete or suboptimal tomorrow. Manually updating prompts to reflect these dynamic changes is a laborious and reactive process, often lagging behind the pace of change. Automation enables prompts to adapt dynamically to changing conditions, by incorporating real-time data, user feedback, and contextual information into the prompt generation process. This allows LLM-powered applications to remain relevant, accurate, and effective over time, without requiring constant human intervention.

The Optimization Challenge:

Crafting effective prompts is an iterative process, involving experimentation and refinement. However, manually evaluating the performance of different prompts and identifying optimal configurations is a time-consuming and subjective task. It is often difficult to systematically explore the vast space of possible prompt variations and identify the most effective prompts for a given use case. Automation provides the tools and techniques for systematically optimizing prompts, by automatically generating variations, evaluating their performance, and identifying the optimal configurations based on predefined metrics. This allows organizations to maximize the effectiveness of their LLM-powered applications and achieve the best possible results.

The Knowledge Management Challenge:

As organizations accumulate a growing library of prompts, managing and sharing this valuable knowledge becomes increasingly complex. Manually documenting and organizing prompts is a tedious and error-prone process, making it difficult for different teams and individuals to discover and reuse existing prompts. This can lead to duplication of effort and a loss of valuable expertise. Automation provides solutions for creating centralized prompt repositories, enabling efficient search, retrieval, version control, and collaboration, transforming prompts into a valuable organizational asset.

This chapter will address these challenges head-on, providing a comprehensive guide to automating and optimizing prompts across the entire prompt lifecycle. We will explore the key technologies, methodologies, and best practices that empower organizations to:

i. **Automatically Generate Prompts**: We will delve into techniques for programmatically creating prompts based on structured data, user input, and predefined templates, eliminating the need for manual prompt crafting.

ii. **Dynamically Manage Prompts**: We will explore strategies for storing, versioning, and retrieving prompts efficiently, ensuring that the right prompt is always available for the right application.

iii. **Continuously Optimize Prompts**: We will examine methods for automatically evaluating prompt performance, identifying areas for improvement, and generating optimized prompt variations.

iv. **Orchestrate Prompt Workflows**: We will investigate techniques for chaining together multiple prompts to create complex, multi-step interactions with LLMs, enabling the automation of sophisticated tasks.

v. **Integrate Prompts into Applications**: We will explore how to seamlessly integrate automated prompt generation and management into existing software systems and workflows.

Let's look at some examples for Automatic Prompt Generation:

We will now delve deeper into the techniques for programmatically creating prompts, showcasing at least five distinct examples relevant to the agile workflow.

Tools Needed:

i. Programming Languages: Python
ii. Data Handling Libraries: Pandas, JSON
iii. Templating Engines: Jinja2
iv. LLM Interaction Libraries: OpenAi (or similar), transformers, cloud-specific SDKs

Example 1: Generating Personalized Product Recommendations

Purpose: To automatically generate diverse and personalized product recommendations based on a richer set of user data, including browsing history, items in their cart, and wish list, in addition to purchase history and stated preferences. This directly supports the Product Owner's goal of increasing user engagement and sales, and requires the Developer to integrate various data sources.

Automation Done: The system aggregates data from multiple user interaction points, selects relevant information, and dynamically populates a more sophisticated prompt template that instructs the LLM to provide a wider range of recommendations with varied justifications.

How to Achieve Automation:

1. Enhanced Data Retrieval: Implement code to fetch a more comprehensive set of user data.

Python

```python
import pandas as pd

user_id = 456
user_data_expanded = {
    'user_id': [user_id],
    'purchase_history': [['book_X', 'gadget_Y']],
    'browsing_history': [['page_A', 'page_B', 'page_C']],
    'cart_items': [['item_Z']],
    'wish_list': [['item_W1', 'item_W2']],
    'preferences': [['science fiction', 'smart home devices']]
}
user_df_expanded = pd.DataFrame(user_data_expanded)
user_ex = user_df_expanded[user_df_expanded['user_id'] == user_id].iloc[0]

purchase_history_str = ", ".join(user_ex['purchase_history'][0])
browsing_history_str = ", ".join(user_ex['browsing_history'][0])
cart_items_str = ", ".join(user_ex['cart_items'][0])
wish_list_str = ", ".join(user_ex['wish_list'][0])
preferences_str = ", ".join(user_ex['preferences'][0])
```

(Tool used: Google Gemini 2.0)

2. More Complex Template: Create a Jinja2 template that utilizes the expanded data.

```python
recommendation_template_expanded = Template("""
Based on the user's past purchases of {{ purchase_history }}, browsing history of {{ browsing_history }},
items currently in their cart: {{ cart_items }}, items in their wish list: {{ wish_list }},
and stated preferences for {{ preferences }}, suggest five diverse and relevant products.
For each suggestion, briefly explain why it might appeal to the user based on this information.
""")
```

3. Prompt Generation: Render the template with the enriched user data.

```python
prompt_expanded = recommendation_template_expanded.render(
    purchase_history=purchase_history_str,
    browsing_history=browsing_history_str,
    cart_items=cart_items_str,
    wish_list=wish_list_str,
    preferences=preferences_str
)
print(prompt_expanded)
```

4. LLM Interaction: Send the generated prompt to an LLM.

```python
response = client.chat.completions.create(
    model="gpt-3.5-turbo",
    messages=[{"role": "user", "content": prompt}]
)

acceptance_criteria = response.choices[0].message.content
print(acceptance_criteria)
```

Relevance to Roles (discussed in this book):

i. **Product Owner**: Uses the generated acceptance criteria as a starting point for defining and refining the conditions of satisfaction for each user story. This ensures clarity and shared understanding within the team.

ii. **Developer**: Relies on well-defined acceptance criteria to guide their development work and to create effective unit and integration tests.

iii. **Scrum Master**: Ensures that user stories have clear acceptance criteria to facilitate effective sprint planning and to track progress during the sprint.

iv. **Agile Leader**: Promotes the use of clear and concise user stories with well-defined acceptance criteria as a key practice for delivering value effectively.

Example 2: Generating Meeting Summaries with Action Item Extraction (Expanded)

Purpose: To not only summarize meeting transcripts but also to automatically extract a structured list of action items with assigned owners and deadlines (if mentioned). This significantly aids the Scrum Master in tracking commitments, the Product Owner in following up on decisions, and the Agile Leader in ensuring accountability.

Automation Done: The system processes the meeting transcript using a prompt that instructs the LLM to identify key discussion points, decisions, and specifically to list action items in a structured format (e.g., "Action Item: [Task], Owner: [Person], Deadline: [Date]").

How to Achieve Automation (for the purpose of consistency in text, the tool used here to show all samples and examples is Google Gemini 2.0):

1. Transcript Acquisition: Assume a system exists to transcribe meeting audio into text. Let's simulate this with a string.

Python

```python
meeting_transcript_expanded = """
Attendees: Alice, Bob, Charlie, Diana.
Topic: Review of Sprint 6 and Planning for Sprint 7.
Alice: Sprint 6 went well, we completed all committed stories.
Bob: However, the deployment took longer than expected.
Charlie: We need to improve our CI/CD pipeline.
Diana: I agree. Let's make that an action item.
Decision: Focus on CI/CD improvement in Sprint 7.
Action Item: Investigate CI/CD pipeline improvements. Owner: Charlie. Deadline: End of next week.
Alice: For Sprint 7, the top priorities are user story #4 and #5.
Bob: I can take on user story #4.
Charlie: I'll start looking at the CI/CD improvements.
Diana: I can work on user story #5.
Action Item: Document the proposed CI/CD improvements. Owner: Charlie. Deadline: Mid of next sprint.
Sprint Goal for Sprint 7: Enhance CI/CD process and deliver key user stories.
"""
```

2. Enhanced Summary Template:

Python

```python
summary_action_items_template = Template("""
Please summarize the following meeting transcript, highlighting the key decisions and the overall goal.
Additionally, extract all action items mentioned in the transcript and list them in the following format:
"Action Item: [Task], Owner: [Person], Deadline: [Date]".

Meeting Transcript:
{{ transcript }}

Summary:
Action Items:
""")
```

3. Prompt Generation:

Python

```
prompt_summary_actions = summary_action_items_template.render(transcript=meeting_transcript_expanded)
print(prompt_summary_actions)
```

4. LLM Interaction and Action Item Parsing:

Python

```
response_summary_actions = client.chat.completions.create(
    model="gpt-3.5-turbo",
    messages=[{"role": "user", "content": prompt_summary_actions}]
)

meeting_output = response_summary_actions.choices[0].message.content
print(meeting_output)

# Further processing might be needed to parse the action items into a structured format
# using regular expressions or more sophisticated NLP techniques.
```

Example 3: Generating User Story Acceptance Criteria with Edge Cases

Purpose: To automatically generate a more comprehensive set of acceptance criteria, including common scenarios and potential edge cases, based on the user story description. This helps the Product Owner define more robust requirements and the Developers build more resilient software.

Automation Done: The system uses a prompt that instructs the LLM to think beyond the basic functionality and consider potential errors, boundary conditions, and alternative flows.

How to Achieve Automation:

1. User Story Input:

```python
user_story_expanded = "As a user, I want to be able to upload a profilepicture so that my profile is more personalized."
```

2. Enhanced Acceptance Criteria Template:

```python
Acceptance_criteria_edge_cases_template = Template("""
Based on the following user story: "{{user_story }}", please generate a ca detailed list of acceptance criteria, including both typical scenarios and potential edge cases.

Detailed Acceptance Criteria:
""")
```

3. Prompt Generation:

```python
prompt_acceptance_edge = acceptance_criteria_edge._cases_template.render(user_story=user_story_expanded)
print(prompt_acceptance_edge)
```

4. LLM Interaction:

```python
response = client.chat.completions.create(
    model="gpt-3.5-turbo",
    messages=[{"role": "user", "content": prompt}]
)

acceptance_criteria = response.choices[0].message.content
print(acceptance_criteria)
```

Example 4: Generating Automated Test Cases from User Stories

Purpose: To automatically generate potential test cases (including input data and expected outcomes) directly from user stories and their acceptance criteria. This aids the Developers and potentially QA testers in creating comprehensive test suites more efficiently.

Automation Done: The system takes a user story with defined acceptance criteria as input and uses a prompt to instruct the LLM to generate a list of test cases that cover the functionality described.

How to Achieve Automation:

1. User Story and Acceptance Criteria Input:

Python

```python
user_story_for_testing = "As a customer, I want to be able to add items to my shopping cart so that I can purchase them later."
acceptance_criteria_for_testing = """
1. Given I am on a product page, when I click the "Add to Cart" button, then the item should be added to my cart.
2. Given I have an item in my cart, when I view my cart, then the item should be listed with its name and price.
3. Given my cart is empty, when I view my cart, then I should see a message indicating that my cart is empty.
"""
```

2. Test Case Generation Template:

```
Summary: Users find the navigation confusing and experience slow loading times, but appreciate the design.

Potential Areas for Improvement:
- Navigation: Re-evaluate the information architecture and user flow to make navigation more intuitive. Consider user testing to identify pain pain points.
- Performance: Investigate the causes of slow loading times and implement optimizations.
```

3. Prompt Generation:

Python

```python
Prompt_test_cases = test_case_template.render(user_story=user_story_for_testing, acceptance_criteria=acceptance_criteria_for_testing)print(prompt_test_cases)
```

4. LLM Interaction:

```
client = OpenAI(api_key=os.environ.get("OPENAI_API_KEY"))

python_response = client.chat.completions.create(
    model="gpt-3.5-turbo",
    messages=[{"role": "user", "content": python_prompt}]
)

nginx_response = client.chat.completions.create(
    model="gpt-3.5-turbo",
    messages=[{"role": "user", "content": nginx_prompt}]
)

generated_python_code = python_response.choices[0].message.content
generated_nginx_config = nginx_response.choices[0].message.content

print("\nGenerated Python Code:\n", generated_python_code)
print("\nGenerated Nginx Configuration:\n", generated_nginx_config)
```
```

By embracing the principles and practices outlined in this chapter, organizations can unlock the full potential of LLMs, transforming them from experimental curiosities into powerful engines of productivity, innovation, and competitive advantage. The transition from manual prompt engineering to automated prompt orchestration is not merely a technical advancement; it is a strategic imperative for any organization seeking to thrive in the age of AI. This chapter provides the roadmap for that transition, empowering you to build the intelligent systems of tomorrow, today. This chapter focuses on the crucial aspects of automating and optimizing prompts to maximize their effectiveness in Agile workflows. As we've seen, well-crafted prompts are essential, but the ability to refine them continuously and automate
```

their use is key to scaling prompt engineering across an organization.

Automatic Prompt Engineering for Agile

Automatic Prompt Engineering (APE) refers to techniques that use LLMs themselves to generate and refine prompts, reducing the need for manual prompt design. This is particularly valuable in Agile, where requirements and contexts can change rapidly.

Prompt Generation with LLMs:

LLMs can be prompted to generate initial prompts based on a high-level description of the desired outcome.

Example:

Prompt: "Generate an exhaustive series of prompts to help a Scrum Master write user stories for an online bookstore feature that allows users to create wish lists." *(N.B.: The Output is going to be large)*

Output:

"General Prompts:

"Write user stories for an online bookstore feature that allows users to create and manage wishlists of books."

"Generate user stories for a wishlist feature in an online bookstore, focusing on the user's ability to add, remove, and view books in their wishlist."

"Create user stories for an online bookstore wishlist feature, including functionality for saving books for later purchase and sharing wishlists with others."

Detailed Prompts:

"As a Scrum Master, write user stories for an online bookstore's wishlist feature, detailing the following aspects:

1. User adding a book to a wishlist from the book details page.
2. User viewing all books in their wishlist.
3. User removing a book from their wishlist.
4. User creating multiple wishlists (e.g., "Want to Read," "Gifts").
5. User sharing a wishlist with friends via email/social media."

"Help me create user stories for an online bookstore wishlist feature with these specifications:

1. The ability for a logged-in user to add a book to a wishlist.
2. The ability for a user to view the books in their wishlist, including

book details (title, author, price, cover image).

3. The ability for a user to remove a book from their wishlist.
4. The ability for a user to move a book from the wishlist to the shopping cart.

“Include stories for error handling (e.g., adding a book to a wishlist when not logged in)."

"Write user stories for an online bookstore wishlist feature, considering these user roles:

1. A registered customer who wants to save books for future purchase.
2. A guest user who wants to be prompted to register/log in when trying to use the wishlist.
3. A user who wants to share their wishlist with others.

Include acceptance criteria for each user story."

Specific Feature Prompts:

"Write user stories for the 'Add to Wishlist' functionality on a book details page in an online bookstore."

"Generate user stories for the feature that allows a user to view the contents of their wishlist in an online bookstore."

"Create user stories for the functionality that enables users to remove books from their wishlists."

"Write user stories for implementing a 'Share Wishlist' feature in an online bookstore."

"Generate user stories for allowing users to create and manage multiple wishlists (e.g., for different occasions or categories)."

Remember to tell the AI to (Yes! Here a LLM is asking you to remember this while talking to an LLM):

1. **Write from the user's perspective.**
2. **Focus on the value the feature provides to the user.**
3. **Use the standard user story format (As a ____, I want to ____, so that ____).**
4. **Include acceptance criteria.**
5. **Consider different user roles or scenarios."**

I know this is overwhelming, but this is just one example as to what extent AI can help you ask the right questions to an LLM. Treat this only as a starting point and apply your thought and knowledge for further refinement.

Prompt Optimization through Feedback Loops:

LLMs can be used to iteratively refine prompts based on feedback. This can involve:

1. Analyzing LLM outputs and identifying areas for improvement.
2. Generating variations of a prompt and evaluating their performance.
3. Using reinforcement learning techniques to train LLMs to generate better prompts.

Example:

Initial Prompt: "Summarize this user feedback."

Feedback Prompt: The summaries are too generic.

LLM-Generated Refinement: "Summarize this user feedback, highlighting specific suggestions for UI improvements and categorizing feedback by feature area."

This creates a closed-loop system for continuous prompt improvement. However, this may not be a single attempt refinement and might need several iterations.

Measuring Prompt Effectiveness in Agile

It's crucial to define metrics to measure how well prompts are performing in Agile contexts. This allows for data-driven optimization.

Relevance: Does the LLM's output address the specific need or task?

Example: When generating user stories, are they relevant to the product backlog and sprint goals? *If not, reiterate the prompt with adjustments with respect to persona patterns, context or clarity of the prompt.*

Accuracy: Is the LLM's output factually correct and free from errors?

Example: When summarizing meeting notes, does the summary accurately reflect the key decisions and action items? *Mitigating bias and ensuring authenticity of the source continue to be a challenge with immense data that the LLMs are trained on.*

Completeness: Does the LLM's output cover all the necessary information?

Example: When generating test cases, does it cover all the acceptance criteria and edge cases?

Efficiency: Does the prompt help to save time and effort?

Example: Does the prompt reduce the time it takes to write user stories or generate reports? *Leverage automated prompting to expedite the process.*

User Satisfaction: Are the users of the LLM's output satisfied with its quality?

Example: Do developers find the generated code comments helpful? Do stakeholders find the generated status reports informative?

Metrics Examples: A team, project manager or any individual may consider the following as good metrics to evaluate the improvements at a Team and Organization level due to implementation of best practices in Prompt Engineering:

i. Time saved in completing a task.
ii. Number of errors or bugs reduced.
iii. User satisfaction ratings.
iv. Code quality metrics (e.g., cyclomatic complexity).

Continuous Improvement of Prompts

Like every event is an opportunity to continuously inspect and adapt to the dynamics of requirements and business, prompt engineering is no different. It's an ongoing process. Agile teams should establish a system for continuously improving prompts. It is recommended to create an individual level, team level or organization level prompt library as a set of reusable templates. Because every prompt will always come out with something seemingly great. But only after several iterations can a user know how much the potential of improvement of the prompt was.

Regular Review: Schedule regular reviews of prompts to assess their effectiveness and identify areas for improvement.

Example: A team that uses LLMs to generate meeting summaries reviews the prompts every few sprints to ensure they are still capturing the most important information.

Feedback Loops: Establish clear feedback loops to gather input from users of the LLM's output.

Example: Developers provide feedback on the usefulness of generated code comments, which is then used to refine the prompt.

Experimentation: Encourage experimentation with different prompting techniques and parameters.

Example: A team experiments with different temperature settings when generating creative ideas to see which setting produces the most innovative results.

Documentation: Document the rationale behind each prompt and any changes made to it. This helps to maintain consistency and facilitates knowledge sharing.

Example: The team maintains a prompt library with descriptions of each prompt, its purpose, and any relevant notes or best practices.

Good to Remember:

1. **Bias is a Lurking Shadow**: Always be vigilant for potential biases in LLM outputs, especially when using complex prompts or generating

content based on external data. Implement rigorous testing and monitoring to identify and mitigate these biases.

2. **Truth Requires Validation**: Never assume the accuracy of LLM-generated content, no matter how sophisticated the prompt. Implement robust verification mechanisms, especially for critical applications, and manage user expectations regarding factual correctness.

3. **Transparency Builds Trust**: Strive for explainability in your prompting strategies. Understand why an LLM produced a particular output, especially in complex scenarios, to facilitate debugging, identify issues, and build user trust.

4. **Security is Paramount**: Treat prompts, especially those involving user input or dynamic generation, as potential security vulnerabilities. Implement thorough input validation and sanitization to prevent prompt injection and other malicious exploits.

5. **Ethics Guides Innovation**: Continuously reflect on the ethical implications of using advanced prompting, particularly in creative domains. Consider issues of authorship, intellectual property, and the potential impact on human skills and creativity. Strive for responsible and ethical AI development practices.

As we conclude this deep dive into the powerful realm of automated and dynamic prompt engineering, it is paramount to temper our enthusiasm with a significant note of caution. The ability to programmatically generate, manage, optimize, and orchestrate complex prompts unlocks unprecedented potential for interacting with Large Language Models (LLMs). However, this advanced capability also introduces a new landscape of challenges and ethical considerations that we, as Scrum Masters, Product Owners, Developers, and Agile Leaders, must navigate with prudence and foresight.

One of the primary areas of concern lies in the potential for unintended consequences and biases. While we strive to create prompts that are objective and aligned with our goals, the underlying LLMs are trained on vast datasets that may contain societal biases related to gender, race, culture, and other sensitive attributes. Advanced prompting, especially when involving intricate chains of instructions or the generation of content based on potentially biased data, can inadvertently amplify these biases in the LLM's output.

For instance, a seemingly innocuous prompt designed to generate job descriptions, if not carefully constructed and tested, might inadvertently favour certain demographics based on historical biases present in the training data. Similarly, prompts aimed at summarizing news articles could, through subtle framing, skew the perceived sentiment or importance of certain events. As Agile Leaders, we must champion a culture of inclusivity and fairness, and this extends to the AI systems we build. Product Owners need to be acutely aware of how LLM outputs might impact their users and ensure that the applications they envision do not perpetuate harmful stereotypes. Developers bear the responsibility of rigorously testing and monitoring the outputs of LLM-powered features for any signs of bias, employing techniques like bias detection and mitigation. Scrum Masters play a crucial role in facilitating discussions around ethical considerations and ensuring that the team allocates time for responsible AI development practices.

Another critical aspect to consider is the issue of verifiability and accuracy. LLMs, even with the most sophisticated prompting, are not infallible sources of truth. They can generate plausible sounding but factually incorrect information, a phenomenon often referred to as "hallucination." Advanced prompting, by its very nature of encouraging more creative and complex outputs, can potentially exacerbate this issue. When we move beyond simple queries and ask LLMs to synthesize information from multiple sources or generate novel content based on intricate instructions, the risk of inaccuracies creeping into the output increases significantly.

Developers must be cautious about directly using LLM-generated content without thorough validation, especially in critical applications. Product Owners need to set realistic expectations with users regarding the accuracy of AI-generated information and implement mechanisms for fact-checking and error reporting. Scrum Masters can help the team incorporate verification steps into their workflow. Agile Leaders should promote a mindset of critical evaluation of AI outputs and emphasize the importance of human oversight, particularly in domains where accuracy is paramount.

Furthermore, the transparency and explainability of LLM behaviour can become increasingly challenging with advanced prompting. As prompts become more complex and involve multiple steps or conditional logic, understanding why an LLM produced a particular output can become opaque. This lack of transparency can hinder our ability to debug issues, identify biases, or even trust the system's decisions, especially in sensitive applications.

Developers should explore techniques for improving the explainability of LLM outputs, such as leveraging attention mechanisms or developing methods to trace the reasoning behind generated content. Product Owners need to consider the user experience implications of potentially unexplainable AI behaviour and design interfaces that provide appropriate context and feedback. Scrum Masters can facilitate discussions on how to balance the power of advanced prompting with the need for transparency. Agile Leaders should advocate for research and development into more interpretable AI models and prompting techniques.

The security implications of advanced prompting also warrants careful consideration. Sophisticated prompts, especially those dynamically generated based on user input, could potentially be exploited by malicious actors to elicit harmful content, bypass safety filters, or even gain unauthorized access to underlying systems if not properly sanitized and controlled.

Finally, the ethical considerations surrounding the automation of creative tasks through advanced prompting cannot be ignored. As LLMs become increasingly capable of generating human-like text, code, and even art, we must grapple with questions of authorship, intellectual property, and the potential impact on human creativity. While advanced prompting can be a powerful tool for augmenting human capabilities, we must ensure that its use does not devalue human skills or lead to the creation of AI-generated content without proper attribution or ethical consideration.

So, if you have reached this far in the book, stay put!

The next chapter brings a lot of insights on the concerns you read about just now.

Chapter 10

Ethical Considerations And The Future Of Prompt Engineering

From the foundational whispers that coax AI into revealing its brilliance, to the intricate dance of crafting precise instructions for Product Owners to sculpt their visions, and finally, empowering our very own coding maestros – the Developers – to wield the power of AI in their daily symphony of creation, testing, and deployment.

Each chapter, a stepping stone, has demonstrated the transformative potential of this rapidly increasing field. Remember the Product Owners, armed with their newfound prompting prowess, shaping user understanding and strategic direction with unprecedented clarity? And our Developers, now equipped to supercharge their workflows, generating code, automating tests, and even orchestrating infrastructure with the intelligent assistance of AI?

Yes, the power is profound, the efficiency gains undeniable.

As we being the final chapter of this book, a crucial question echoes in the digital ether: with such power at our fingertips, **what are our Responsibilities?**

Just as a master craftsman understands the ethical implications of their creations, so too must we, the architects of prompts, navigate the ethical terrain that comes with wielding such influence over intelligent systems.

This isn't just about writing clever instructions; it's about shaping the future of how we interact with AI, ensuring fairness, transparency, and accountability in an increasingly agile world.

This concluding chapter addresses the critical ethical considerations surrounding prompt engineering in Agile and looks ahead to the future trajectory of this rapidly evolving field. As we've explored the power of prompt engineering to transform Agile practices, it's imperative to ground our enthusiasm in a framework of responsibility and foresight.

Ethical Considerations in Prompt Engineering

The integration of prompt engineering and LLMs into Agile workflows introduces a range of ethical challenges that require careful attention. These challenges span various domains, from data bias to job displacement.

Bias and Fairness

The Problem: LLMs are trained on massive datasets that may contain inherent biases reflecting societal inequalities related to gender, race, ethnicity, religion, sexual orientation, and other protected attributes. Prompts can inadvertently amplify these biases, leading to unfair or discriminatory outcomes.

Example:

Prompt: "Generate user personas for a new loan application system."

Ethical Issue: The LLM might generate personas that stereotype certain demographic groups as higher or lower credit risks, perpetuating existing biases in lending practices.

Mitigation Strategies:

Data Auditing: Carefully audit the training data used to develop LLMs to identify and mitigate biases.

- **Prompt Engineering for Fairness:** Design prompts that explicitly instruct the LLM to avoid biased outputs and consider diverse perspectives.
- **Bias Detection and Correction:** Implement mechanisms to detect and correct biased outputs from LLMs.

- **Human Oversight:** Maintain human oversight in critical decision-making processes to ensure fairness and prevent algorithmic discrimination.

Transparency and Explainability

The Problem: LLMs are often "black boxes," meaning it's difficult to understand how they arrive at specific outputs. This lack of transparency can erode trust and make it challenging to identify and correct errors or biases. In Agile, where collaboration and understanding are key, this is a significant concern.

Example:

Prompt: "Prioritize the following user stories based on business value."

Ethical Issue: If the LLM provides a prioritization without explaining its reasoning, the Product Owner may not be able to validate the decision or understand why certain stories were prioritized over others.

Mitigation Strategies:

Explainable AI (XAI) Techniques: Employ XAI techniques to make LLM decision-making processes more transparent.

Chain-of-Thought Prompting: Encourage the LLM to show its reasoning steps.

Documentation: Maintain thorough documentation of the prompts used and the LLM's outputs.

Human-in-the-Loop Systems: Incorporate human review and feedback into the process to ensure that the LLM's outputs are understandable and justifiable.

Privacy and Data Security

The Problem: Prompt engineering often involves processing sensitive data, such as user information, code, or business strategies. It's crucial to protect this data from unauthorized access, use, or disclosure.

Example:

Prompt: "Generate code for handling user authentication."

Ethical Issue: The prompt or the LLM's output might inadvertently expose sensitive information, such as API keys or database credentials, if not handled carefully.

Mitigation Strategies:

Data Minimization: Only provide the LLM with the minimum amount of data necessary for the task.

Data Anonymization and Pseudonymization: Remove or obscure personally identifiable information (PII) before processing data with LLMs.

Secure Data Handling: Implement robust security measures to protect data during transmission, processing, and storage.

Privacy-Preserving Techniques: Explore techniques like federated learning or differential privacy to enable LLMs to learn from data without directly accessing it.

Job Displacement

The Problem: The automation capabilities of prompt engineering and LLMs raise concerns about potential job displacement, particularly for tasks that involve repetitive or rule-based work.

Example:

Prompt: "Generate a significant portion of the boilerplate code for a new web application."

Ethical Issue: This could reduce the need for junior developers who primarily handle such tasks.

Mitigation Strategies:

Upskilling and Reskilling: Invest in training and development programs to help workers acquire new skills that are in demand in an AI-driven economy.

Human-AI Collaboration: Focus on how humans and AI can work together synergistically, with AI augmenting human capabilities rather than replacing them entirely.

Job Creation: Recognize that AI can also create new jobs in areas such as prompt engineering, AI maintenance, and AI ethics.

Social Safety Nets: Explore social safety net policies to support workers who are displaced by automation.

Misinformation and Manipulation

The Problem: LLMs can be used to generate convincing but false or misleading information, which can be used to manipulate public opinion or spread misinformation.

Example:

Prompt: "Generate a persuasive argument against a particular product or company."

Ethical Issue: This could be used to create fake reviews or spread negative propaganda.

Mitigation Strategies:

Fact-Checking and Verification: Implement mechanisms to verify the accuracy of information generated by LLMs.

Watermarking and Provenance Tracking: Develop techniques to track the origin and authenticity of AI-generated content.

Media Literacy Education: Educate the public about the potential for AI-generated misinformation and how to critically evaluate information.

Responsible AI Development: Promote the development and deployment of LLMs in a responsible and ethical manner.

Environmental Impact

The Problem: Training and running large LLMs requires significant computational resources, which consume energy and contribute to carbon emissions.

Example:

Training a very large LLM requires massive data centres and can have a substantial energy footprint.

Ethical Issue: Companies need to consider the environmental impact of their AI development and deployment.

Mitigation Strategies:

Energy Efficiency: Develop more energy-efficient LLM architectures and training methods.

Renewable Energy: Power data centres with renewable energy sources.

Sustainable AI Practices: Adopt sustainable AI practices that minimize the environmental impact of AI development and deployment.

Carbon Offsetting: Invest in carbon offsetting projects to compensate for carbon emissions.

AI Laws and Regulations Worldwide

The rapid advancement of AI has prompted governments and regulatory bodies around the world to develop laws and regulations to address the ethical and societal challenges posed by this technology. This section provides an overview of key AI laws and regulations, with a focus on their implications for prompt engineering in Agile.

European Union: The AI Act

Overview: The EU AI Act is one of the most comprehensive and ambitious attempts to regulate AI. It takes a risk-based approach, categorizing AI systems into different risk levels and imposing corresponding requirements.

Key Provisions:

Prohibited AI Practices: The Act prohibits certain AI practices that are considered to pose an unacceptable risk, such as cognitive behavioural manipulation and untargeted scraping of facial images.

High-Risk AI Systems: AI systems that pose a high risk to people's health, safety, or fundamental rights are subject to stringent requirements, including risk assessments, data governance, transparency, and human oversight. Examples include AI used in critical infrastructure, education, employment, and law enforcement.

Limited-Risk AI Systems: AI systems that pose a limited risk are subject to transparency obligations, such as informing users that they are interacting with an AI system.

Minimal-Risk AI Systems: AI systems that pose minimal risk are generally not subject to specific regulations.

Implications for Prompt Engineering in Agile:

Prompt engineering for high-risk AI systems (e.g., AI used in hiring tools within Agile HR practices) will need to be carefully designed to meet the Act's requirements for fairness, accuracy, transparency, and robustness.

Documentation of prompts and their outputs will be crucial for demonstrating compliance with the Act's transparency obligations.

Agile teams will need to incorporate ethical considerations into their development processes, including risk assessments and bias mitigation strategies.

Example:

If an Agile team is developing an AI-powered tool to assist with employee performance evaluations, the AI Act would classify this as a high-risk system. The prompts used to generate evaluation criteria, analyze employee data, and generate feedback would need to be carefully designed to avoid bias and ensure fairness. The team would also need to document the prompts and the system's decision-making process to comply with the Act's transparency requirements.

Reference:

European Commission - Proposal for a Regulation laying down harmonised rules on artificial intelligence (Artificial Intelligence Act) and amending certain union legislative acts: This is the official document outlining the AI Act.

United States

The US approach to AI regulation is more fragmented than the EU's, with various agencies and initiatives addressing specific aspects of AI. There is no single, comprehensive federal AI law yet, but there is growing momentum towards more structured regulation.

Key Initiatives and Guidance:

AI Risk Management Framework (AI RMF) by NIST: The National Institute of Standards and Technology

(NIST) has developed the AI RMF, a voluntary framework to help organizations manage AI risks and promote trustworthy AI.

NIST AI Risk Management Framework:

https://www.nist.gov/itl/ai-risk-management-framework

Blueprint for an AI Bill of Rights: The White House Office of Science and Technology Policy (OSTP) has released a Blueprint for an AI Bill of Rights, which outlines principles for protecting individuals' rights in the age of AI.

Blueprint for an AI Bill of Rights:

https://www.whitehouse.gov/ostp/ai-bill-of-rights/

Agency-Specific Regulations: Various federal agencies, such as the Federal Trade Commission (FTC) and the Equal Employment Opportunity Commission (EEOC), are issuing guidance and enforcing existing laws to address AI-related issues within their respective jurisdictions.

Implications for Prompt Engineering in Agile:

Agile teams in the US should familiarize themselves with the NIST AI RMF and the AI Bill of Rights to ensure that their AI systems are developed and deployed in a trustworthy and ethical manner.

Prompt engineering practices should align with principles of fairness, transparency, and accountability.

Agile teams should be aware of agency-specific regulations that may apply to their AI systems, such as regulations related to consumer protection, employment discrimination, or healthcare.

Example:

If an Agile team is developing an AI-powered customer service chatbot, they should consider the FTC's guidance on truthfulness in advertising and avoid using prompts that could lead the chatbot to make misleading or deceptive claims. They should also implement mechanisms to ensure that the chatbot respects user privacy and handles personal information securely.

China

China has been actively developing AI regulations, with a focus on both promoting AI innovation and managing its potential risks.

Key Regulations:

Regulations on the Management of Algorithmic Recommendations on Internet Information Services: These regulations govern the use of algorithms to recommend content to users, aiming to protect users' rights and interests.

Measures for the Management of Deep Synthesis Internet Information Services: These measures regulate the use of deep synthesis technologies (e.g., deepfakes), requiring providers to label deep synthesis content and prevent its misuse.

Implications for Prompt Engineering in Agile:

i. Agile teams developing AI systems for recommendation algorithms or deep synthesis applications in China must comply with the relevant regulations.
ii. Prompt engineering practices should consider the regulations' requirements for transparency, user rights, and content labelling.
iii. Ethical considerations, such as preventing the spread of misinformation and protecting user privacy, are crucial.

Example:

If an Agile team is developing an AI-powered news aggregation application in China, they need to ensure that the recommendation algorithms used by the application comply with the regulations on algorithmic recommendations. The prompts used to generate summaries or categorize news articles should avoid promoting biased or misleading content.

OECD AI Principles: The Organisation for Economic Co-operation and Development (OECD) has developed a set of principles for trustworthy AI.

UNESCO Recommendation on the Ethics of Artificial Intelligence: The United Nations Educational, Scientific and Cultural Organization (UNESCO) has adopted a recommendation on the ethics of AI, providing a global framework for ethical AI development and deployment.

Best Practices for Ethical Prompt Engineering in Agile

To navigate the ethical challenges and comply with emerging regulations, Agile teams should adopt the following best practices for prompt engineering:

Establish an Ethical Framework

Develop a clear set of ethical principles and guidelines for AI development and prompt engineering within the organization.

These principles should address key ethical concerns, such as fairness, transparency, privacy, and accountability.

Involve stakeholders from diverse backgrounds in the development of the ethical framework.

Example: An Agile team developing an AI-powered hiring tool adopts ethical principles that prioritize fairness, non-discrimination, and transparency in the hiring process.

Conduct Ethical Risk Assessments

Conduct thorough ethical risk assessments before and during the development of AI systems that involve prompt engineering.

Identify potential ethical risks, such as bias, privacy violations, or misuse, and develop mitigation strategies.

Regularly review and update the risk assessments as the AI systems evolve.

Example: An Agile team assesses the risk of bias in the training data used to develop an LLM for generating customer service responses and implements data augmentation techniques to balance the dataset.

Prioritize Data Quality and Diversity

Ensure that the data used to train and evaluate LLMs is of high quality and represents the diversity of the user population.

Address data gaps and biases to minimize the risk of unfair or discriminatory outcomes.

Implement data governance policies to manage data collection, storage, and use responsibly.

Example: An Agile team carefully curates a dataset of user feedback to train an LLM for sentiment analysis, ensuring that the dataset includes feedback from users of different demographics and backgrounds.

This isn't just a theoretical dossier. It's a practical guide to navigating the ethical complexities of this powerful technology in the real world of agile development. Just as we wouldn't send our self-driving car onto the road without understanding the rules and potential hazards, we cannot unleash the full potential of Prompt Engineering without a deep understanding of its ethical dimensions. So, let's embark on this final leg of our journey, not with caution, but with mindful awareness and a commitment to shaping a future where the power of AI, guided by ethically sound prompts, truly empowers us all. The road ahead is exciting, but it demands our thoughtful and responsible navigation. Let's ensure we drive it well.

Closing Notes

A Symphony Of Ingenuity

As we draw this exploration of prompt engineering in Agile to a close, it's vital to recognize the profound shift we stand at the cusp of. This book has endeavoured to be more than a guide to techniques; it has aimed to illuminate a pathway toward a future where Agile's inherent adaptability is amplified by the boundless potential of Artificial Intelligence. We've journeyed from the foundational principles of crafting effective prompts to the cutting edge of AI agent development, and in doing so, we've uncovered a transformative force poised to reshape the very essence of how we build and deliver value.

The chapters have meticulously detailed how prompt engineering empowers each key player in the Agile ecosystem. Scrum Masters can orchestrate more efficient ceremonies, Product Owners can articulate product vision with unprecedented clarity, and Developers can transcend the limitations of manual coding, becoming architects of innovation. Agile Leaders, armed with AI-driven insights, can navigate complexity with foresight and chart strategic courses previously obscured by the fog of uncertainty. This is not merely about automating tasks; it's about augmenting human capabilities, freeing us from the mundane to focus on the truly meaningful – the strategic, the creative, and the human-centric.

Yet, the true power of prompt engineering lies not in its individual applications but in its holistic integration into the Agile philosophy. Agile, at its core, is a symphony of collaboration, adaptation, and continuous improvement. Prompt engineering provides the instruments, the scores, and even the conductor to elevate this symphony to new heights of harmony and effectiveness.

Imagine:

- **Self-Evolving Agile Processes:** AI agents constantly analyzing team interactions, identifying bottlenecks, and dynamically adjusting workflows to optimize flow.
- **Proactive Risk Mitigation:** LLMs scanning the horizon for potential disruptions, predicting roadblocks, and generating mitigation strategies before they impact the project.
- **Hyper-Personalized User Experiences:** AI-driven insights gleaned from user feedback, translated into rapid iterations of product features that anticipate and exceed customer expectations.

This is the promise of Agile AI – a dynamic partnership where human intuition and ingenuity intertwine with the computational power and pattern recognition of Large Language Models.

However, this transformative power comes with a weighty responsibility. The ethical considerations we've explored – bias, transparency, privacy, and the potential for societal disruption – are not mere footnotes; they are the very foundation upon which we must build this future.

The AI laws and regulations emerging across the globe are not obstacles to innovation but guardrails to ensure that this technology serves humanity. Embracing ethical frameworks, conducting rigorous risk assessments, prioritizing data quality, and designing for transparency are not optional add-ons but essential components of responsible Agile AI development. We must cultivate a culture of ethical awareness, where every prompt is crafted with consideration for its potential impact, and every AI system is deployed with a commitment to fairness and accountability.

The journey ahead will undoubtedly be filled with challenges. The technology will continue to evolve at a breakneck pace, demanding constant learning and adaptation. New ethical dilemmas will emerge, requiring innovative solutions and collaborative dialogue.

Yet, the potential rewards are immense.

We've together spent a huge part of our book learning how to build and expertly drive a magnificent, self-driving car. We've mastered the controls, understood its capabilities, and even customized it to perfectly navigate the bustling highways of agile product development. We know how to program its destination, optimize its route for speed and efficiency, and even instruct it to adapt to changing traffic conditions. It's a marvel of engineering, capable of taking us to our goals faster and more smoothly than ever before.

But now, I would like to take your imagination to something important, before we close.

Imagine you are onboard a self-driving car hurtling down a busy street. We, the prompters – the programmers of its journey – have meticulously set its course. But what if our initial programming, our prompts, inadvertently lead it down a path that, while efficient, cuts corners on safety? What if the data we fed it to learn the rules of the road contained biases, causing it to react differently to certain types of pedestrians or other vehicles? What if the very speed and efficiency we optimized for come at the cost of predictability and transparency, making it difficult to understand why it made a particular decision in a critical moment?

Suddenly, the thrill of speed and efficiency takes a backseat to the weight of responsibility. We realize that simply knowing how to drive the car isn't enough. We need to be deeply aware of the ethical implications of its operation. We need to consider the safety of everyone on the road, the fairness of its decision-making, and the transparency of its actions. We need to establish clear ethical guidelines and constantly evaluate whether our programming aligns with these principles.

This, my friends, is precisely where we find ourselves with Prompt Engineering in the agile world.

We've learned to harness the immense power of AI through carefully crafted prompts. We've witnessed its ability to accelerate our development cycles, enhance our understanding, and even automate complex tasks.

But the agile nature of our work – the constant iteration, the rapid feedback loops, the collaborative ways of working – amplifies the importance of embedding ethical considerations into our prompt engineering practices from the very beginning.